A
QUESTION
OF
FAITH

A
QUESTION
OF
FAITH

An Atheist and a Rabbi
Debate the Existence of God

cʒ cʒ ঽ০ ঽ০

William E. Kaufman
and
Morton Shor

JASON ARONSON INC.
Northvale, New Jersey
London

Library of Congress Cataloging-in-Publication Data

Kaufman, William E.
    A question of faith : an atheist and a rabbi debate the
existence of God / by William E. Kaufman and Morton Shor.
      p. cm.
    Includes bibliographical references and index.
    ISBN 1-56821-089-2
    1. God (Judaism) 2. God—Proof. 3. Atheism. I. Shor, Morton.
II. Title.
BM610.K395   1994
296.3'11—dc20   93-34034

Manufactured in the United States of America. Jason Aronson Inc. offers books and cassettes. For information and catalog write to Jason Aronson Inc., 230 Livingston Street, Northvale, New Jersey 07647.

To Nathalie and Sylvia
and especially to the memory of
the late Dr. Saul A. Wittes,
who was the catalyst of our dialogue

Contents

Part III Epilogues

Acknowledgments

We want to thank Carl Zukroff, Graphic Project Manager in the School Division of Houghton Mifflin Company, for his advice and suggestions.

We have been enriched by our respective families. The rabbi is indebted to his wife, Nathalie, for her love and support, to his son, Ari, for his penetrating questions, and to his daughter, Beth, Assistant Editor, College Division, McGraw-Hill, for her wise suggestions on how to improve the manuscript.

Mort Shor is grateful to his wife, Sylvia, for her love and support.

We also wish to thank our editor, Arthur Kurzweil, and Muriel Jorgensen and Janet Warner of the staff of Jason Aronson Inc. for their help, care, and sage guidance throughout the creation of this book.

And we thank those who typed the manuscript at various stages of its development, Louise Keane, Jan Partington, and Lori Kokoszka.

Introduction

One of the issues most vital to human existence is that of God's nature and existence. Wars have been fought and lives have been lost over religious contentions. This is the "black book" of religion, its negative effect in history.

Religion's positive aspect is that ideas of God have inspired great philosophies, fostered magnificent works of art, and, according to some thinkers, have laid the foundations for ethics and values.

The problem of God is of philosophical, psychological, historical, and anthropological interest. It tells us much about human beings and their hopes, fears, and aspirations. Recently, God has become a hot topic for some scientists, as theoretical physicists have begun to wrestle with the science–religion interface and metaphysical questions concerning the origin of the universe and the conception of a cosmic mind.

Our interest is primarily philosophical and theological. The purpose of this book is to present the issue of God's nature and existence in a dispassionately intellectual manner but also

in a lively style—namely, in the form of a correspondence between a rabbi and an atheist. The best format for an issue as
controversial as ours is a debate, where both sides can be deline-
ated, and a debate in the form of letters adds the flavor and
seasoning of real life situations to the argumentation.

Notice that our topic is the *nature* and existence of God.
Philosophers today agree that the problem of God's nature
logically precedes the issue of Divine existence, since people
must have a concept of what they are talking about before they
can reasonably discuss the Deity's existence. Gather ten people
in a room and ask them what their conception of God is, and
you are likely to receive ten different answers. That is why it
is important to be clear about the various theological options,
the differing ways people conceive of God's nature.

This book is addressed to both the Jewish and the general
reader and to both an academic and a popular audience. Since
we are, respectively, a rabbi and a Jewish atheist, understand-
ably there will be references to theological options in contemporary Jewish thought. Since the rabbi holds a doctorate in
general philosophy and teaches philosophy of religion in a
college, however, he is aware of present trends in this area and
guides the discussion toward overall as well as specifically Jewish theological philosophical issues.

What are the theological options? First, there is classical theism—the concept of God as an omnipotent (all-powerful), omniscient (all-knowing), and perfectly good Being. A troublesome
obstacle here is the Holocaust. Some continue to hold classical
theism, leaving the question how an omnipotent, perfectly good
Deity could allow such a catastrophe to the unfathomable will
of God. Others, however, introduce revisionary or alternative
concepts of God. One is limited theism: God is a perfectly good
Being but not omnipotent. Another is religious naturalism. According to some religious naturalists, God is not a personal Being

but the sum total of all the creative processes in nature. Others, known as process theologians, envisage God as a cosmic mind in process with the universe, guiding creatures with persuasive but not coercive power.

Mort Shor, on the atheistic side, rejects both the classical and the revisionary notions of God. He compares *all* ideas of God with the concept of a seven-legged dog or a unicorn. His point is that concepts of God are irrational, that there is no more reason to believe in God than in the existence of a seven-legged dog.

Needless to say, this claim leads to an extremely lively debate and correspondence. It's up to the reader to decide whether the rabbi or the atheist has the stronger case.

We hope this book will enable the reader to discover new ways of looking at the questions about which, above all, we seek illumination: What are we talking about when we talk about God? And *does God exist?*

I

PROLOGUES

1

Atheist's Prologue

What makes an atheist? When my friend Bill Kaufman asks me when I became an atheist, I respond that I really do not know. Then I add, "Why do you believe?" His reply is simple and straightforward (I paraphrase): "Because of my upbringing. Because of the influence of my mother."

My atheism is certainly not due to my upbringing. Although I recall the few childhood encounters with religion as negative, I cannot really attribute my skepticism to these experiences. (I also cannot state at what point I said to myself, "God is a fiction.")

One of my earliest memories is the death of a younger brother during the diphtheria epidemic of 1923, when I was about four-and-a-half years old. I have a vague memory of my mother's hysteria and her angry denials of God. There could be no God, she said, if her little son could be taken. I never learned if my mother's rejection of God was something of the moment or if my brother's death had really made her an atheist. Religion was not a

3

subject that was discussed in our house. My mother still bought only kosher food and kept separate dishes for meat and dairy.

My father was a kind, gentle man, religiously observant but tolerant. He prayed at home every morning wearing phylacteries and a prayer shawl and attended services at the local synagogue on Saturdays and, of course, on the High Holy Days. He was a strange mixture of religious orthodoxy, tolerance, and plain common sense. His common sense told him that the reasons for the religious ban on shellfish no longer existed, and oysters, clams, and lobster were just too delicious to avoid. So shellfish it was, but outside the house.

Both of my parents emigrated from Poland. As was the Jewish custom of the time, they sent their young son to learn Hebrew from a *melamud*, a private Hebrew teacher. I remember this tyrant was a heavily bearded, black-clothed, humorless individual who reeked of tobacco and worse. He wielded a stick with which he rapped my knuckles every time I misread or hesitated over a word. At one point, he missed my knuckles and struck my wrist with such force that he smashed my watch. At the tender age of nine or ten I was not famous for my gentleness or forbearance. In my fury, I drew myself up to my full four-foot-something, spat into the face of the astonished teacher, called him a "lousy son of a bitch," and ran all the way home in tears. When my father returned from work that evening, I expected the heavens to open and inundate me with the most drastic of punishments. To my utter astonishment, my father listened to my story and calmly said that I need not return to the *melamud*.

I was not what one would call an easy child. In fact, as far back as I can remember, I was known as a kind of holy terror (perhaps holy is the wrong adjective). Now I like to think of my young self as an individual or independent. I really was just plain ornery. Further evidence of my nonconformism appeared on the occasion of my *bar mitzvah*. At that time, it was customary for the *bar mitzvah* to make a speech, preferably in Yiddish. The speech should have been highly stylized and composed of thank you's to the relatives for the gifts and thank you's to the parents for helping the *bar mitzvah* to reach "manhood." I rejected the idea that at thirteen I was a man and added that I would convey my thank you's personally. Again, my father showed his open-mindedness and went along with my wishes.

Having become a *bar mitzvah*, I was supposed to say prayers several times a day, the first before breakfast. This went on for about two months, and one day I said that I had had enough. I could not see the point, so I just stopped. (To this day, I do not see how I continued for the two months.) I expected reprimand (at least) or punishment (at most) for my refusal to continue. Again, my father surprised me by saying that it was my decision to make. And that was my last direct personal involvement with God and religion.

During the era of the Great Depression I was a normal adolescent: I rebelled. I rebelled against everything that was "Establishment," but mostly I rebelled against religion. I flirted with the simplistic political, economic, and social solutions that were current at the time. Upon attaining maturity, however, all of these nostrums quickly lost their appeal. My skepticism about religion and blind faith, however, developed into a firm atheism.

After several false starts in higher education, I enrolled in the School of Technology of the City College of New

York, and in the early 1940s I graduated with honors with the degree of Bachelor of Chemical Engineering. I worked in war-related projects until the end of World War II but left the field to go into the family business with my father and older brother. There, I oriented the business from the horse-and-buggy era to the new high-tech world. In 1988 I retired, and I now live in Northern Westchester County in New York State. I am active in the local chamber music society and do volunteer work at a state prison.

My original correspondence with Rabbi William Kaufman started after the death of my dear friend and brother-in-law, Saul, who had been a member of Rabbi Kaufman's Woonsocket, Rhode Island, congregation. The occasion of our meeting was Saul's death, but the impetus to write was the reading of Dr. Kaufman's book, *Contemporary Jewish Philosophies*. There was so much in the book that I objected to and disagreed with, so much that I considered irrational, illogical, unrealistic, and unsound, that I wrote Dr. Kaufman a letter (of I don't recall how many pages) taking issue, point by point, with scores of statements in the book. Of course, he replied, and thus began a correspondence that started as "Dear Rabbi"–"Dear Morton" and soon became "Dear Bill"–"Dear Mort." The dialogue soon settled into a debate over the existence of God. It continued for about two years and petered out in 1987.

In the fall of 1990, stimulated by Richard Friedman's *Who Wrote the Bible?* and Harold Bloom's *The Book of J*, I was perusing the Pentateuch. I was baffled by the meaning of Exodus 4:24 to 4:26. In these verses, Moses is on his way back after his self-exile from Egypt. He stops at an inn with his wife and infant son. God appears and wishes to kill Moses. His wife, Zipporah, circumcises their son, places the foreskin at Moses' feet, and says, "Thou art my blood bridegroom." God then decides that He will let Moses live. Why did God wish to slay Moses? What was the significance of the infant's circumcision? What was the meaning of Zipporah's words? These questions and a myriad of others raised by these strange passages were thrown at my old friend Bill. In response to my questions, Rabbi Kaufman sent me a rather abstruse explanation printed by a seminary. The important part of this reply, however, was his suggestion that we cooperate on a book that he was writing. It was to be called *The Case for God*. With me on the team, however, the title was changed to *The Case for and against God*. Of course, I jumped at his suggestion, and we renewed our correspondence, *ab ovo*.

At the outset, Bill asked me if I intended to prove that God does not exist. My response was that one cannot prove that anything does not exist. I said I cannot prove that a seven-legged dog does not exist. The burden of proof must be on the positive; Bill must prove that God *does* exist.

In our face-to-face discussions, I postulated the situation of the little green man from outer space coming to Earth and dropping in on Friday night services at Bill's synagogue. He observed the prayers to God and asked, "God? What is that? Who is that?" He was given any one (or all) of the definitions, descriptions, and explanations that various theologians propound. His natural questions were, "Why do you believe these things? Do you have any evidence to support these pictures of God that you have shown me? Why are there so many different answers to the question of what God is? Upon what do you base all of this?" He quietly listened to the attempts to answer his questions, and then he pulled on the leash of his seven-legged dog and returned to his spaceship for the voyage home.

2

Rabbi's Prologue

The atheist's challenge activated dormant doubts. The crucial event had been the shattering of my naive childhood faith, the collapse of my belief in the "picture" of God as a cosmic bookkeeper. (By a "picture," I mean a worldview, a way of construing events, an explanatory style, a conceptual framework for understanding and interpreting life.) The earliest such picture in my life, and the most pervasive in Judaism, is precisely this notion of God.

As children, we learn to think and talk about God from religious traditions. In Judaism, the most familiar part of the tradition is embodied in the *Mahzor*, or High Holy Day prayer book for Rosh Hashanah (the New Year) and Yom Kippur (the Day of Atonement). God is pictured in the High Holy Day liturgy as the Supreme Judge. Like a shepherd who gathers his flock, God is depicted bringing forth every human being for review, determining his or her destiny for the coming year. According to the Jewish tradition, on Rosh Hashanah "it is inscribed," and on Yom Kippur "it is sealed, who shall live and who shall die. . . , who shall be at ease and who shall be afflicted, who shall be brought low and who shall be exalted."

But repentance, prayer, and righteousness can avert the severe decree. In Judaism, as in Christianity, God is portrayed as this cosmic bookkeeper who keeps a record of virtues and vices. In Christianity, Christ offers vicarious atonement for sin to the faithful Christian. Divine judgment and retribution for the unrepentant sinner are the motifs of Western religion.

This entire world-picture collapsed for me when my mother, Betty, an extremely pious woman, died of cancer at fifty-two. Watching her waste away those final months of 1959 filled me with anger against the alleged justice of the divine decree. In particular, I remember, she tried to put on her glasses to read and recite a traditional prayer called *Ashrei*. (*Ashrei* means "happy.") The prayer begins, "Happy are those who dwell in Thy house; they will ever be praising Thee." Unfortunately, my mother's face was so shrunken from the cancer that the glasses kept falling off her face. Unable to contain my rage, I left her bedside and went into my room. Taking a prayer book, I opened to the page of the *Ashrei* prayer and, weeping in anguish, ripped up the *siddur*.

The tearing of this sacred book when I was twenty represented a rupture in my life of faith. Never again, I thought, would my faith be whole, implicit, unconditional, or totally accepting. A first-year student in rabbinical school, I would start searching for a new "picture," a new way of understanding Judaism and the world.

After my mother died, I felt at first a strange affinity with the cold desert landscape of the absurd of Camus, the lonely atheistic existentialism of Sartre, the bleak emptiness of the agnostic Bertrand Russell's universe. But these feelings were profoundly depressing. So I held fast to the study and practice of Judaism with the hope that some residue of faith would be rekindled. I attended the daily prayer services, faithfully reciting the Mourner's *Kaddish*.

At one of these services, I discovered a new insight into my mother's prayer. Verse 10 of the *Ashrei* states, "All thy works shall give thanks unto Thee, O Lord; and thy loving ones shall bless Thee." An instructive comment explains:

> Judaism bids man bless God's name for the evil, as for the good, that may befall them. "The Lord gave, and the Lord hath taken away; blessed be the name of the Lord" (Job 1: 20). Resignation to God's will is as much a duty as is thanksgiving for His unending mercies. Every creature shows some gratitude for any good that befalls it; but it is only the *hasidim*, "those who love God," that *bless* His name even in the darkness of woe, sorrow, and suffering.[1]

I found in the foregoing comment another way of looking at my mother's death. Instead of cursing the darkness, perhaps I could kindle a light? Instead of railing at the alleged injustice of God, I could think of my

---

1. *The Authorized Daily Prayer Book*, rev. ed. Hebrew text, English translation with commentary and notes by Dr. Joseph H. Hertz, the late chief rabbi of the British Empire (New York: Bloch Publishing Co., 1948), p. 87.

mother as one of the *hasidim* (the pious ones), as a kind
of saint, as one who loved God and was striving to bless
God's name even in the darkness of her suffering. Perhaps she had attained a level of piety that only religious
virtuosi attain, such as the second-century sage Rabbi
Akiba, who died with the words "Hear O Israel, the Lord
our God, the Lord is One" on his lips as the Romans
combed his flesh with iron. Rabbi Akiba's death by mar-
tyrdom was the true fulfillment of the command
to love God with all your soul—even if He takes your soul.

But I could not hold to this view of acceptance con-
sistently. To attribute my mother's death to the will of
God opened up a theological can of worms—in particular, the "monotheistic syndrome" and the problem of
evil. If God is both omnipotent and perfectly good, why
do the righteous have to suffer at all? Why are there
"natural" evils like cancer and "moral" evils such as the
Holocaust? But suppose God is not omnipotent. What's
limiting Him? And isn't a finite, limited God a contradiction in terms? If God is not in complete control, why
worship Him?

A mystic once said that a God we could comprehend
would not be a God. Perhaps our concepts shatter when
we try to understand God. But perhaps there is nothing
to understand, so why believe in God at all? Why believe in the "Big Maybe"? If it is just a plunge of irrational faith, a leap into the dark to feel some sense of
comfort, is it even worth seeking? So I was open to Mort
Shor's challenge to determine if belief in God can stand
the test of intellectual scrutiny.

Another factor predisposing me to this openness was
the memory of my father. Harry Kaufman worked as a
mechanical engineer for the Philadelphia Naval Base.

Born in South Philadelphia, the oldest of three children, Harry did not have the financial backing to explore careers. Shouldering the responsibility for the family, he was compelled to work during the day and studied accounting and engineering at night. He never passed the C.P.A. exam, so accounting remained a part-time job. And once he attached himself as an engineer to the Philadelphia Naval Base, there, to the chagrin of my mother, he remained for the rest of his working life. My mother's unfulfilled ambition for my father displaced itself onto me; I had to redeem the family.

My parents were a union of irreducibly opposed natures. Whereas my mother was a pious believer, adhering rigidly to the rituals of Judaism, my father was an agnostic whose religion was literature. In every spare moment, he was either reading or writing. One of my most indelible childhood memories was returning home after Sabbath services to find my father smoking a cigar and typing an article, both activities being forbidden on the Sabbath by Jewish law. My father's wide readings in secular and scientific literature had led him to reject a naive belief in a supernatural Deity who "commanded" ritual observance. My mother was, of course, enraged at my father's open defiance, but he retorted that a humanistic ethic was far more important than slavish obedience to ritual. Invariably, he would point to Jews who would adhere to every iota of ritual law but, in business, would employ all sorts of sharp practices to cheat their fellow man.

The conflict between my parents was a major chronic circumstance of my life. Like Goethe's Faust, "two souls dwelled within my breast"—the simple piety of my mother versus the questioning skepticism of my father.

My father expired from congestive heart failure at the age of sixty-two, 8 years after my mother's death. My interest in philosophy and theology can in part be attributed to my effort to resolve that representational conflict between faith and skepticism.

One thing I wanted to discover through dialogue with Mort Shor was whether my belief in God was merely a product of cultural conditioning, stemming from the rigid (but loving) guidance of my mother, who wanted to see her son "make it" as a rabbi to compensate for her husband's failure (in her eyes) to "make something of himself." Or perhaps my belief in God stands up under scrutiny and represents a live, compelling, and rationally justified intellectual option.

By "rationally justified" I do not mean to imply that the existence of God can be proved. Rather, I mean that it is a belief that a rational person would accept. An entire philosophical literature on the meaning of rationality and the question of whether belief in God is rational now exists. There are, as always, many philosophers who are atheists. But there are also first-rate philosophers who argue that it *is* rational to believe in God.[2]

First, however, we must determine what we mean by "God," which logically precedes the question of existence. The problem is that the word *God* is ambiguous. In the Bible, "God" is a proper name. God in the Hebrew Bible is an individual, a spiritual person whose character is portrayed in words and deeds. He is a Being to whom it is appropriate to pray. He speaks to Moses; He loves His people Israel; He gets angry at them when they

---

2. The names of Charles Hartshorne, Alvin Plantinga, and Richard Swinburne come to mind.

worship the Golden Calf. In the New Testament, the focus shifts to the incarnation of God in Jesus. In both testaments, God is intensely personal.

Under the influence of the Greeks, the medieval philosophers began to think of God *generically.* The Greeks were the first people to raise generic questions such as What is matter? What is mind? and What is godhood? Thus, instead of being anthropomorphically conceived, God became a generic concept, and philosophers began to ask the question, What is the *nature* of God?

The definition of God in accordance with classical theism is an omnipotent (all powerful), omniscient (all-knowing), perfectly good Being, who is the Creator of the universe. But if God is omnipotent and perfectly good, why is there evil? If He is omnipotent, He *could* prevent evil. If He is perfectly good, He *would* prevent evil, as in the case of the Holocaust, where eleven million died at the hands of the Nazis.

The tendency to redefine God as "limited" and not omnipotent is testified to by the immense popularity of Harold Kushner's book, *When Bad Things Happen to Good People.* There is a variety of God-concepts that limit God's power and emphasize God's goodness, such as the notion of God as the sum total of creative goodness in the world (religious naturalism) and God as the Universal Mind in process with the universe, having persuasive but not coercive power (process theology).

Four major theological alternatives may be noted:

1. The God of the Bible: creator, personal, anthropomorphic (pictured in human form), causing things to happen directly, giving free will to human beings, rewarding and punishing.

2. The God of classical theism: infinite, unlimited, omnipotent, omniscient, omni-benevolent Being, creator of all things, causing some things directly and others indirectly, endowing human beings with free will.

3. The God of religious naturalism: the sum total of all creative goodness in the world, unified in one creative Force, not a personal Being.

4. The God of process theology: the Universal Mind in process with the universe, having persuasive but not coercive power.

Given these options, we need a working concept for the debate with atheism. I suggest "a unitary actuality which is supremely worthy of worship and/or commitment.[3] This is nicely inclusive because it explains the plethora of contemporary God-concepts: theologians differ on which idea of God is supremely worthy of worship. Some maintain that only an omnipotent God is worthy; others say a perfectly good God limited in power deserves our worship; and others, such as feminist theologian Dorothy Soelle, emphasize the caring aspect of a God who is with us in our suffering. Like the process theologians, she does not attribute coercive power to God.

This abundance of God-concepts seems like an invitation to the destructive ax of the atheist. Sigmund Freud, for example, theorized that God was a magnified father figure, a cosmic projection, and therefore an illusion. Feminist theologians, however, have as much justifica-

---

3. I owe this definition to the process theologian John B. Cobb, Jr.

tion in portraying a goddess as men do in thinking masculine.

Freud's argument proves nothing, however. Although ideas of God are projections of the human mind, it is still logically possible that there exists a unitary actuality—a God—who created this projective mechanism in the human mind. In fact, the only thing Freud's theory does show is that most people do need a kind of heavenly parent or cosmic protector. In one sense, I admire the atheist who claims that he or she does not need it. But human need is only the beginning as we seek a truthful and open dialogue with the atheist. Our aim is to determine whether or not there are good reasons to believe in the existence of a Higher Power.

I attract atheists, I think, because I am a rabbi and may be easy to tease (fair game, etc.). But I like to think it's because I am open-minded and amenable to discussion and argument. My first confrontation with an atheist was with Tom in the summer of 1975. Tom actually looked like Mephistopheles, with his dark beard and steel-blue eyes. I met him at the Nantasket Beach, Hull, Massachusetts, where both our families spent many summers. We would walk the beach arguing about God summer after summer, sometimes accompanied by Tom's large but jovial dog, Bertha. When I became annoyed at Bertha's loud barking, Tom would say ironically, "She's God's creature!"

A former professor of philosophy and currently a professor of government, Tom is Jewish by birth but dissociated himself from all aspects of theology and heritage. He could be brutally sarcastic. One summer I came to the beach limping, recovering from a broken ankle suffered the previous February. Tom's first remark when he saw me was, "Look what Yahweh (the God of Hebrew Scriptures) did to you!" In his more serious moments, however, Tom exhibited a finely tuned logical mind. The author of a book on logic, he gave me a complimentary copy and inscribed it with the words: "To Bill, who already seems to me to be more logical than is good for his soul."

This master of logic suggested a clever distinction between *interesting* and *credible* theologies. The notion of an omnipotent, omniscient God who intervenes in the course of events he called "interesting" because, if true, it really made a decisive difference in the world. The plain man's God (a combination of the biblical God and the God of classical theism, to whom it would make sense to pray) is interesting but not very credible. On the other hand, strictly philosophical concepts of God (such as the religious naturalist who redefines God as the unity of the creative forces in nature) are credible because there are, indeed, creative forces working in nature. But such an idea is not very interesting because it doesn't make much difference in the conduct of life. The challenge of theology, Tom claimed, was to develop and articulate a concept of God *both* interesting and credible.

Rick was a less flamboyant atheist. A professor of philosophy at the University of Massachusetts, Dartmouth, he emphasized the importance of not jumping to conclusions and being patient with the atheist's viewpoint. He pointed out how interesting the philosophical issues underlying the theist–atheist debate were. For example, he noted the claim of the agnostic British philosopher Bertrand Russell that the universe is just *there*, as a brute fact. I used to think that this was impossible. Like most people, I thought there had to be a reason for everything. Rick said that the idea that everything has a reason or explanation is controversial, the subject of a contemporary philosophical debate concerning the status of the principle of sufficient reason. Is the status of this principle psychological or real?

Finally, there is my present "opponent," Mort Shor, who is older and more intensely scientific than the others. Also, he is more respectful of religious traditions—in particular, of his own Jewish heritage. Mort's essential point is that there is no more reason to believe in God than in imps, fairies, or a seven-legged dog. I am presently in the lion's den with him.

I think that our debate is an important contest. In an interesting, aptly titled book *The Religious Significance of Atheism*, the French philosopher Paul Ricoeur concluded that atheism's religious significance is, "An idol must die, in order that a symbol of Being may speak."[4]

The Jewish religion began when Abraham shattered the idols of his father, Terach. There are many God-concepts—like God as cosmic bellhop who magically answers all prayers—that are indeed idolatrous. The diatribes of the atheist can have religious significance by eliminating idolatrous concepts of God and thereby paving the way for purer God-ideas.

In short, I see the atheist as offering an important challenge to the theist. One of the things I seek to learn through this dialogue is the religious significance of Mort Shor's atheism.

---

4. Alasdair MacIntyre and Paul Ricoeur, *The Religious Significance of Atheism* (New York: Columbia University Press, 1969), p. 98.

II

THE CORRESPONDENCE

3

Introductory Comment to the Correspondence

Our correspondence was renewed when Mort came across a puzzling biblical passage while reading *The Book of J*,[1] the audacious work of literary restoration by Harold Bloom, claiming that the oldest of the several texts of the Torah referred to by scholars as J was written by a woman. The passage that disturbed Mort seems to depict Yahweh's attempt to murder His prophet Moses. (The name Yahweh refers to the biblical God of Israel.) "What kind of a God is this?" Mort asked himself as he read the following passage:

> On the way, at a night lodging, Yahweh met him—and was ready to kill him. Zipporah [Moses' wife] took a flinty stone, cutting her son's foreskin; touched it between Moses' legs: "Because you are my blood bridegroom." [Yahweh] withdrew from [Moses]. "A blood bridegroom," she said, "marked by this circumcision."[2]

---

1. *The Book of J*, translated from the Hebrew by David Rosenberg, interpreted by Harold Bloom (New York: Grove Weidenfeld, 1990).
2. Ibid., p. 144.

This is one of the passages that persuaded Bloom that J was a woman, because Zipporah, the wife of Moses, stands up against Yahweh. But a prior question agitated Mort: "What kind of a God is this? Demonic, capricious, uncanny, irrational?" The enigma here is Yahweh's motive.

The most cogent explanation of this incident is as follows. Whereas polytheistic literature would attribute the experience to a demonic being, Israelite monotheism admits of no independent forces other than the one God. The biblical scholar Nahum Sarna suggests that (contrary to *The Book of J*) it was Moses' firstborn son, Gershom, who was stricken and *not* Moses. Zipporah, the mother, attributed her son's illness to uncircumcision. The biblical scholar explains that Moses may well have neglected this ritual because of the danger of exposing a newly circumcised boy to the rigors of the journey through the wilderness.

In any event, Mort's questions about this passage introduce the major issue of the correspondence: the nature and existence of God. The issue is, first, what is the *nature* of God? Is God a personal Being who claims absolute obedience to His laws, as described in the foregoing biblical passage? Or is God an impersonal cosmic force, as suggested by many philosophers? If God is personal, is God omnipotent, as depicted in the Bible? Or is God good but limited by the forces of chaos and evil, as suggested by the popular book *When Bad Things Happen to Good People*, by Harold Kushner. Second, is God *real*? Does any kind of a God—a Being, Force, or whatever—actually exist? And why should we believe that God exists? Is there any evidence? How do we know? Are the biblical narratives evidence? Or is it all a matter of faith?

Through our exchange, we seek the truth, insofar as it is possible for human beings to gain insight into these profound matters.

4

Why Is There a Need for a God?

March 21, 1991

Dear Mort,

The questions you raised concerning Exodus 4:24, 25, 26 are answered in the enclosed photocopy.

Much more interesting to me, however, is the possibility of resuming our correspondence.

Do you still maintain as you did previously that you know of no need for God and do not recognize such a need?

I look forward to hearing from you.

With warmest best wishes.

Sincerely,

Bill

March 26, 1991

Dear Bill,

Many thanks for your so-prompt reply to my inquiry about Exodus 4:24 to 26. I found it fascinating.

I was delighted to learn that you are interested in resuming our correspondence (discussion? discourse? difference?) about God.

In your letter you ask if I still maintain that I know of no need for God and do not recognize such a need. No, Bill, I do not feel any need for God nor can I recollect ever having felt such a need. On the other hand (and here, admittedly, I have changed my view 180 degrees) I believe that most people do have a need to believe. And not just a need but a hunger, a craving—and for two separate reasons: the here-and-now and the hereafter.

Thoreau said, "The mass of men lead lives of quiet desperation." For the oppressed and the dispossessed, life can be a daily struggle to maintain a life which is really a meaningless existence. I refer here to the peoples of the Third World; to peoples ground down by tyrannies; the underclasses of the Western world; the great mass of people who greet each new day with no more hope for a better life than they had on the previous day. For these people belief is relief. God (and all of the religious concomitants) can give meaning to lives which would otherwise be empty. God (through His agents) can give meaning to life and make it seem worthwhile.

Even among the fortunate, the peoples of the Western world who have achieved some degree of economic security and political freedom, life can lack meaning but for other reasons: crass materialism, smug self-absorption, Babbittry, hedonism—and the realization and recognition of all of this. When our successful Madison Avenue executive suddenly comes face-to-face with the meaninglessness and emptiness of his life, where can he turn? Obviously, he turns to God because He can give him meaning and purpose in his life. And that is the first need fulfilled by God, the "here-and-now" need.

As for the "hereafter," at some point in his travels between birth and death, man is suddenly faced with the realization that after he has put in his three-score-and-ten he will disappear into oblivion. He will quickly fade away as have the untold millions before him (as well as the untold millions to follow). At this point, the thinking man starts asking questions. Why am I here? What purpose do I have in life? Does life have any meaning? How can I, the center of the universe, die? How can the universe continue after I die? What is it all about? And on and on and on.

If our subject believes in God, he has a kind of answer to all of his questions.

Belief in God commonly implies a belief in the immortal soul! and the hereafter. As a matter of fact, *The New York Times* of March 23, 1991, reported that the latest Gallup poll of American adults showed that 78 percent believe in an eternal reward (read: Heaven) for people who lead "good" lives, and 60 percent believe that eternal damnation (read: Hell) awaits those who led "bad" lives and died without repenting. God tells the believer that life has meaning and is worth living.

Voltaire must have been aware of this when he said, "If God did not exist it would have been necessary to invent Him." And that is just what man has done because of his dire need for Him.

Now, of course, you will ask, "If God gives such comfort and such meaning to man, why deny Him?" My answer is simply that God is an anodyne for those who need Him. Let those who need Him have Him, but let us recognize God for what He is. An anodyne is an anodyne.

Well?

Your friend,

Mort

P.S. Of course, my use of the words *he, him, his, man,* etc., is not intended as sexist but is merely a convenience.

5

Did God Create Us
or Did We Invent God?

INTRODUCTORY COMMENT TO THE ARGUMENTS
FOR THE EXISTENCE OF GOD

In the Bible, the existence of God is assumed; it is not a matter for
argument or doubt. In the ancient biblical world, the existence of God
or gods was as real to people as electricity is to us. The major question then was *Which* God is the true Deity? The belief in one universal God (monotheism) who is supreme over nature and history constituted the revolution of ancient Israelite monotheism. When the
Psalmist observed, "The fool hath said in his heart 'There is no
God'" (Psalm 14:1), he was referring not to disbelief in God's existence but to the denial of God's moral governance of the world.

Abstract philosophical speculation was foreign to both the authors
of the Bible and the rabbis of the Talmud and *Midrash*. Only under
the stimulus of Greek and Islamic philosophy did philosophical speculation arise among Jews in the Middle Ages. Medieval Jewish philosophy concentrated heavily on problems concerning the existence
and nature of God. And a major task of philosophical theology was

the attempt to prove God's existence. These attempted proofs, or arguments, for the existence of God are thus the logical starting point for discussion about God.

To begin with, it is important to observe that the object of these arguments is to prove the existence of the God of classical theism. *Theism* is generally contrasted to *deism*. *Deism* refers either to the idea that an "absentee god" long ago set the universe in motion and thereafter let it alone or, historically, to the position of the eighteenth-century English deists, who taught that natural theology (that theological truths can be worked out by the unaided human reason without recourse to biblical revelation) alone is sufficient. By contrast, *theism* refers to the belief in a personal Deity.

Classical theism refers to the traditional, standard concept of God in Judaism, Christianity, and Islam, that is, a person without a body (a spirit) who is eternal, perfectly free, omnipotent, omniscient, perfectly good, and the creator of the universe. These qualities attributed to God are known as the *Divine attributes*. Some of these attributes require explanation. "Eternal" means that God always existed and always will exist. God's being "perfectly free" means that no object or event or state of affairs causally influences God to act. God's own choice at the moment of action determines what God does. "Omnipotent," or all-powerful, signifies that God is able to do whatever is logically possible for God to do. Similarly, "omniscient," or all-knowing, means that God knows whatever is logically possible for God to know.

As we shall see, there are other types of theism. For example, *limited theism* asserts that God is perfectly good but not omnipotent. However, for our present purposes, let us bear in mind that the object of the traditional arguments for the existence of God refers to the God of classical theism.

Before introducing the arguments for the existence of God, let's be clear about the meaning of the term *argument*. *Argument*, in this context, does *not* mean an altercation with one's spouse. Rather, *argument* is a term of logic, that branch of philosophy that deals with the identification of correct versus incorrect reasoning. Some preliminary terms first need to be defined.

A sentence is a group of words that means something intelligible. There are different kinds of sentences. An *imperative*, for example, is a command (e.g., "Shut the door."). Arguments, however, deal with *declarative* sentences containing a subject and a predicate. What interests the logician is not the grammar of the sentence but what the sentence asserts. What the sentence asserts is called a *statement* or *proposition*. A proposition or statement is said to be true or false.

An *argument* is a group of propositions of which one, the conclusion, is claimed to be true on the basis of other propositions, the *premises*, which are asserted as providing grounds or reasons for accepting the conclusion. There are two types of arguments. A *deductive* argument is one whose premises are claimed to provide conclusive grounds for the truth of its conclusion. The classic example is:

1. All men are mortal.
2. Socrates is a man.
3. Therefore, Socrates is mortal.

This is a valid argument; if the premises are true, the conclusion is true also, and the conclusion thus follows from the premises. The argument is also sound; both the premises and the conclusion are true.

Many arguments are not claimed to demonstrate the truth of their conclusions as following necessarily from their premises but are intended merely to support their conclusions as probable or probably true. Arguments of this type are called *inductive*. For example:

1. Every swan I have ever seen is white.
2. Therefore, the swan I will see tomorrow is white.

It is logically possible that I might see a black swan tomorrow, but this is extremely improbable. Thus, the premise supports the probable truth of the conclusion.

Most of the arguments for the existence of God infer His existence from some feature of the universe (e.g., its order). The most purely deductive proof for God is the ontological argument. This attempted proof tries to establish that solely from the definition of a Supreme Being, it follows that God must necessarily exist. It is an *a priori* piece of reasoning; no knowledge about the world is required to develop the argument. (*A priori* means, literally, prior to experience, as opposed to *a posteriori*, based on experience.)

The ontological (from the Greek *ontos*, meaning being) argument originated with St. Anselm (1033–1109), Archbishop of Canterbury in England. Naturally, St. Anselm believed in God as a matter of faith. But his was a faith seeking *understanding*; he wanted to employ reason to understand what he was believing. Anselm contended that anyone who understood what was meant by the term *God* or *Supreme Being* would see that such an entity must exist. "God" is that Being of which none greater can be conceived: a GCB, or greatest conceivable Being. Because we can comprehend this definition, we can conceive of God. Furthermore, we can conceive of God as existing not only as a concept in our own minds but also as existing in reality, independently of our ideas. Because it is greater to exist both as an idea *and* as a real thing than merely to exist as an idea, God must exist both in reality and as an idea, for by definition God is that Being of which nothing greater can be conceived. Another way of phrasing the argument is to define God as the most perfect Being. A most perfect Being, by definition, includes all perfections—all good qualities or predicates. One such quality is existence. Therefore, God or a most perfect Being exists.

There have been many critiques of this form of the ontological argument. One is that existence is not a predicate or quality. The first critic was Gaunilon, a monk at Marmontiers, France, and a contemporary of Anselm. He claimed that Anselm's reasoning leads to absurd conclusions. Gaunilon pointed out that if this sort of reasoning were legitimate, one could show that all kinds of unreal or imaginary objects must exist. Someone could imagine, for example, that there is a perfect island somewhere beyond the point where any explorer could possibly go. It would follow, from Anselm's reasoning, that if one could conceive of such an island, it must exist. Criticisms like this tended to show that, contrary to Anselm, God cannot be defined into existence. Just because we can conceive of something, like a unicorn, doesn't mean it exists in reality.

Anselm's reply to Gaunilon gives rise to his second form of the argument. In his response, Anselm differentiated between the concept of God and the idea of a most perfect island. The idea of God is unique; it contains something that is lacking in the idea of a most perfect island. That element is *necessary existence.*

Here a crucial distinction occurs. The island, or any material object, is part of the *contingent* world. *Contingent* means dependent on other things, referring to something that didn't have to exist. We human beings are examples of contingent beings; we are dependent on the oxygen in the environment, for example. Furthermore, but for our parents, we might not have existed. God, by contrast, has necessary existence. God is totally independent; He has *aseity,* or self-existence (from the Latin *a se,* "from itself"). Anselm's point is a subtle one, namely, God cannot be conceived of as not existing. If we think of God as not existing, we are not thinking of God.

Still, even though this second form of the argument is more clever than the first, most philosophers nevertheless object to it also. The crux is the concept of necessary existence. Philosophers generally accept the idea that there are necessary truths (such as A = A or 2 + 2 = 4), but many of them claim that to attribute necessary existence to something is to mix apples and oranges. The term *necessary* has a legitimate application to statements, but applying it to individual existence is what philosophers call *controversial;* some philosophers accept it, whereas others declare it a meaningless conjunction of words. Thus, most philosophers find the ontological argument inconclusive.

The other arguments for the existence of God are *a posteriori*, or empirical; they begin from facts of our experience. Two of these arguments are *cosmological* (from the Greek *cosmos*, meaning world), from features of the world that allegedly point to God. To begin with, there is the argument for a First Cause. From what we observe, we see things move, change, or happen. In order for these events to occur, there must be a cause, either a prior event or a reason for the occurrence of the event. As we trace back effects to their causes, there is either an infinite regress (we can continue indefinitely) or a First Cause or Ultimate Explanation that requires no further cause or explanation.

Most people balk at the idea of an infinite regress. They think, It has to stop somewhere! Thinking of an infinite regress—spatial edgelessness or temporal endlessness or beginninglessness—can be dizzying. The contemporary Jewish philosopher Martin Buber reported that when he was fourteen, such reflections about the edge of space or its edgelessness, or time with and without a beginning or end, almost drove him to suicide.[1] So it is understandable why people generally feel that we must stop somewhere, or that there must be an Ultimate Explanation. The general principle underlying this intuition is known as PSR, or the *Principle of Sufficient Reason*. This is the principle that there must be an explanation of the existence of any being or of any positive fact whatever.

Let us test this principle. Suppose you say to a child, "God created the world," and the child then inquires, "Well, who created God?" Stuttering and stumbling, you say, "God always was" or some similar remark. But, in fact, the child may be on to something. Philosophically, the status of the principle of sufficient reason is con-

---

1. Martin Buber, *Between Man and Man*, trans. Ronald Gregor Smith (New York: Macmillan, 1978), p. 136.

troversial; it isn't clear whether it's just a necessity in our minds that there must be a First Cause or Explanation or a necessity in reality. Reality, or nature, is not bound to satisfy our presuppositions. And perhaps the universe itself is a brute fact and there is no explanation.

Thus, this form of the cosmological argument is inconclusive because it depends on one's intuition. Some, probably most, people intuit that there must be a First Cause; others may have no problem with an infinite regress. Perhaps the medieval Catholic philosopher Thomas Aquinas realized that a stronger cosmological argument was necessary, and he therefore developed his "Third Way": the argument from contingency.

Remember that the term *contingent* means "dependent on other things for existence" and refers to something that might not have existed. Everything we observe in the world is contingent, that is, it is true of each item that it might not have existed at all. The fact is that, for everything we observe, there was a time when it did not exist. This printed page, for example, did not always exist; it is a product of lumberjacks, transport workers, paper manufacturers, and so on. Thus, if everything were contingent, there would have been a time when nothing existed. But then nothing could have come to exist (*ex nihilo nihil fit*—out of nothing, nothing can come). But there *are* things in existence. Therefore, there must be something that *has* to exist, that is *noncontingent*, that has necessary existence—and this is what we call God. Only a self-existent reality, containing in itself the source of its own being, something outside the system of the universe or universes, can thus constitute the ultimate ground of existence.

Here too, however, the atheist can reply, "Why can't *everything* be contingent? Maybe the universe is just a brute fact. Why does the universe have to be intelligible?" This is one of the apparent stalemates between the theist and the atheist. What we have are two competing intuitions: the theist's intuition that the universe must be intelligible and the atheist's opinion that "it ain't necessarily so."

Finally, there is the famous design, or teleological (from the Greek *telos*, meaning end or aim), argument. Suppose you are walking on the beach and you see a rock. You may properly attribute its existence to chance—to random operations of natural forces such as wind, rain, heat, volcanic action, and the like. Walking further along the beach you see a watch lying in the sand. You cannot reasonably account for its existence by recourse to chance, for a watch is intricately structured, consisting of a complex arrangement of wheels, cogs, axles, balances, and springs. The only way to account for the watch is to postulate an intelligent mind or designer.

Now, the universe is as complex—indeed infinitely more complex—than the mechanisms of the watch. Moreover, the universe seems calibrated for life's existence. There are simply too many coincidences. For example, if the force of gravity were pushed upward a bit, stars would burn out faster, leaving little time for life to evolve on the planets circling them. Moreover, if the relative masses of protons and neutrons were changed by a hair, stars might never be born, because the hydrogen they need wouldn't exist. If at the time of the Big Bang some basic numbers (the initial conditions) had been juggled, matter and energy would never have conjugated into galaxies, stars, or planets stable enough for life as we know it. In short, the essence of the teleological argument is that the universe is simply too fine-tuned for human life to be a product of chance. Rather, all of these "coincidences" point to a cosmic designer or architect—God.

Another apparent stalemate in the theist–atheist debate is the atheist's contention that if you let simple molecules reshuffle themselves randomly for long enough, some complex ones would get formed, like DNA, a stable self-replicating molecule. If for the atheist the key word is *chance*, for the theist it is *purpose*. What does it all *mean*? To the theist there is meaning and purpose in the cosmos. We human beings belong here; we were *intended*. The atheist does not deny that we, as individuals, can shape our lives into a meaningful, purposeful existence. What the atheist denies is the theist's insistence that there is a cosmic underlying reason, purpose, or intelligence directing things, or simply at work in some way, in nature and in human life.

We are now in a position to reflect on Rabbi Kaufman's schematized form of the arguments, which he utilizes in his university philosophy classes, and the atheist's response to them. We shall see that none of the arguments individually constitutes a decisive proof. The crucial issue is whether the data of all the arguments, taken together, represent a cumulative case for the existence of God. In other words, when we consider the factors of causation, order, design, and human consciousness, do all of these taken together point inductively to the probable existence of a Supreme Being as the best explanation for these phenomena?

We suggest that you take a piece of paper and draw a line down the center. In one column, place all considerations and data that you think point to the existence of God, and in the other column list those data and considerations that negate it. Keep this pad of paper by your side, adding to it as you read the letters.

ଓ ଓ ଡ଼ ଡ଼

April 1, 1991

Dear Mort,

I was delighted to learn that you also are interested in resuming our correspondence.

The main point you made in your letter was your observation that God is an anodyne. Webster's dictionary defines "anodyne" as anything that relieves, lessens, or soothes pain. The claim that God is an anodyne re-echoes Karl Marx's thesis that belief in God is the opiate of the masses and is similar to Freud's claim that religion is an illusion and that God is a psychological projection of the image of a father figure.

The fact is that religion has always served two purposes: to comfort the disturbed and to disturb the comfortable. You have emphasized one at the expense of the other. If you read the Hebrew prophets such as Jeremiah and Isaiah you will see that much of their message was to disturb the comfortable—i.e., to shatter the complacency and awaken the conscience of those who attend the Temple service on the Sabbath and cheat their fellow human beings during the week. In this connection the aim of the prophets was to heighten, not lessen, the pain of conscience in the people.

The main issue that you pose, however, is whether God is merely an idea or a reality. Did man invent God or did God create man? Is God real or merely a psychological projection?

Once a week I teach a course in philosophy at Rhode Island College. In this course, we discuss the arguments philosophers have developed for the existence of God. The purpose of these arguments is to demonstrate that God is real, that God as the Supreme Being exists.

Enclosed is a sketch of the main arguments. A more detailed statement of the arguments is given in the book I sent you some time ago: *Philosophy of Religion*, by John Hick.

What do you think about these arguments? Even if you find individual fallacies in the separate arguments, don't all the arguments, taken together, suggest to you the probability that God exists as the First Uncaused Cause and the source of order and purpose in the universe? How else can you explain the order in the universe?

I look forward to hearing your response.

Your friend,

Bill

Definitions

1. The Ontological Argument: an *a priori* argument (purely conceptual, prior to experience). If we understand the meaning of "God" as the GCB, the greatest conceivable Being, we will intuitively understand that a GCB or most perfect Being must exist (ontological from Greek *ontos*, meaning being).

2. The Cosmological Arguments: *a posteriori* arguments (based on experience) attributing features of the world (from Greek *cosmos*) to God.
   a. PSR: the principle of sufficient reason (everything that happens has an explanation).
   b. Contingent: ontologically dependent.

3. The Teleological Argument: an argument from design or purpose (Greek *telos*, meaning end or purpose).

Arguments for the Existence of God

A. Ontological Argument—an *a priori* argument developed by Anselm:
   1. The term *God* means a being of which none greater can be conceived (a GCB or a most perfect Being).

2. Suppose a GCB exists only in the mind.

3. Then it is possible to conceive of a yet more perfect Being that exists in reality as well as in the mind.

4. Therefore, God or a GCB exists.

B. Cosmological Argument—an *a posteriori* argument developed by Aquinas, the First Cause Argument:

1. Everything that happens has a cause or explanation (PSR).

2. This cause in turn must have a cause.

3. The series of causes must either be infinite or have its starting point in a first cause.

4. An infinite regress of causes is impossible.

5. Therefore, God or a First Cause exists.

C. Cosmological Argument—an *a posteriori* argument, Aquinas' Third Way, the argument from contingency:

1. Some contingent beings exist.

2. Contingent beings require a noncontingent ground of being in order to exist.

3. Therefore, God or a noncontingent ground of being exists.

D. Teleological Argument—the *a posteriori* argument from design:

1. Nature exhibits a number of instances of means ordered to ends.

2. The ordering of means to ends presupposes the existence of an intelligent designer.

3. Therefore, the ordering of means to ends in nature presupposes the existence of God or an intelligent being by whom all natural things are directed to their end or purposes.

❈ ❈ ❈ ❈

April 4, 1991

Dear Bill,

I'm sorry that I cannot give a concise reply to your April Fools' Day missive, but I'll try not to be too wordy.

Even if, as you say, religion serves two purposes (comforting the disturbed and disturbing the comfortable), this does not in any way invalidate Marx's or Freud's theses. The "masses" are certainly not comfortable; and religion can serve both purposes and still be an illusion.

But that has little bearing on our differences about God. So let me take up your four arguments for the existence of God.

First we have Anselm's ontological argument:

1. The term *God* means a being of which none greater can be conceived (a GCB or most perfect Being).

2. Suppose a GCB exists only in the mind.

3. Then it is possible to conceive of a yet more perfect Being that exists in reality as well as in the mind.

4. Therefore, God or a GCB exists.

The fallacy here is easily shown if we replace God with any other imaginary thing, such as a dog with seven legs.

Then we have the cosmological argument, the First Cause argument of Aquinas:

1. Everything that happens has a cause or explanation.

2. This cause in turn must have a cause.

3. The series of causes must either be infinite or have its starting point in a first cause.

4. An infinite regress of causes is impossible.

5. Therefore, God or a First Cause exists.

There are two fallacies in this argument: First, statement no. 4 is an assumption unsupported by any verifiable evidence. And second, statements nos. 1 and 5 contradict each other.

The cosmological argument, or the argument from contingency, runs as follows:

1. Some contingent beings exist.

2. Contingent beings require a noncontingent ground of being in order to exist.

3. Therefore, God or a noncontingent ground of being exists.

The fallacy here is similar to the fallacy in the First Cause argument. The argument is based upon the unsupported assumption that (to paraphrase) an infinite regress of things is impossible.

Finally, we have your teleological argument, or the argument from design.

1. Nature exhibits a number of instances of means ordered to ends.

2. The ordering of means to ends presupposes the existence of an intelligent designer.

3. Therefore, the ordering of means to ends in nature presupposes the existence of God or an intelligent being by whom all natural things are directed to their end or purposes.

This argument seems to put the cart before the horse. For example, the believer says that the ozone layer is a perfect example of God's existence. How could this layer of gas be just the right composition, just the right thickness, and in just the right place to shield all living things on Earth from lethal ultraviolet rays from the sun? It is too much of a coincidence to have happened by pure chance. With equal logic, one can say that the earth happened to have an ozone layer of such a nature that living things could exist there. That is a much simpler approach.

Finally, Bill, you ask if these arguments, taken together (despite some fallacies), suggest the probability of the existence of God as a First Cause. The answer is a resounding NO! The sum of four false arguments is not a true argument. Also, let us not confuse probability with possibility. How do I explain the order of the universe? There is no independently verifiable evidence of God or a First Cause, and I cannot explain the order of the universe. By analogy to the ozone layer argument, we might say that were there not this system and order in the universe, the universe would not exist.

Lacking an explanation, however, I will not invent fairies or elves or God (or dogs with seven legs).

All the best,

Your friend, Mort

6

The Plain Man's God (the God of Classical Theism) as the Object of the Traditional Arguments

April 9, 1991

Dear Mort,

In his claim that religion is an illusion, Freud meant that it originates in the human mind as a psychological crutch, a product of a wish or fantasy and a projection of a father image. The origin of an idea is not an index of its truth, however. To assert this is to commit the genetic fallacy. For it is logically possible that in his work on the father image, Freud may have discovered one of the mechanisms by which an actually existent God creates an idea of Deity in the human mind.

Before I comment on your response to the classical arguments for the existence of God, it is important to discuss the meaning of the word *God*.

The idea of God that is the object of the traditional arguments is known as the God of classical theism. I call it the plain man's God. You call it the Big Guy. The classical theist defines "God" as "a person without a body (i.e., a spirit) who is eternal, perfectly free, omnipotent (able to do whatever is logically possible for an all-powerful Being to do), omniscient (knowing whatever is logically possible for an all-knowing Being to know), perfectly good, and the creator of all things."

In our time, however, there are various alternative conceptions of God that have been developed. In subsequent letters, I shall describe these alternative concepts. Because of the variety of concepts of God, I suggest as a minimal definition of God "a unitary actuality that is supremely worthy of worship." Would you agree to this definition?

Getting back to the arguments, bear in mind that what they are trying to prove is the existence of God of classical theism (the Big Guy). Most philosophers recognize that there are fallacies in these arguments (which is one reason why some have developed alternative God concepts), but the arguments are not as easily disposed of as you have done.

First, Anselm's ontological argument. When Anselm developed this argument, a contemporary of Anselm, a monk named Gaunilon, criticized it along the lines that you have, saying that you could just as easily prove the existence of a most perfect island or, as you say, a seven-legged dog. Anselm answered Gaunilon in what has come to be known as the second form of the ontological argument. A most perfect island or a seven-legged dog can, without contradiction, be thought of as not existing.

Unlike a seven-legged dog, however, the idea of God is that of a Being who has *necessary existence*, that is, if we get the idea of God correct, we will see that He *has* to exist for if He did not exist, He wouldn't be perfect.

The fallacy of this argument is that it assumes that existence is a predicate that necessarily belongs to God. It isn't. The only logical conclusion is that *if* God exists, He is self-existent or self-caused.

This brings us to the First Cause argument. You are quite right here that an infinite regress is possible. Your claim that the argument from contingency is based on the impossibility of an infinite regress is not correct, however. The idea of this argument is that only a self-existent reality, containing *in itself* the source of its own being, can constitute an ultimate ground of the universe.

And consider what you are left with. Your claim vis-à-vis the teleological argument is that the entire universe is a product of chance. I am willing to admit that there are chance factors in the universe. But the overwhelming order in the universe has to be accounted for; it cries out for an explanation.

My claim is that all the arguments taken together, in addition to the religious experiences of humankind, constitute a cumulative case for the existence of God, if not an omnipotent Being, at least a Higher Power or intelligence, a unitary actuality, that is worthy of worship.

I look forward to hearing from you.

                              Your friend,

                              Bill

April 13, 1991

Dear Bill,

When I referred to Freud's calling religion an illusion (in mine of April 4) I did not mean to imply that his thesis and his explanation thereof made it a fact. I was simply expressing my (admittedly unsupported) view, in common with your views on God and religion. I feel that Freud was quite correct but I cannot cite independently verifiable proof. (I love those last three words!)

What you call the "plain man's God" or the God of classical theism is probably the God of the vast majority of mankind. (This raises still another question in my mind. By what right do you modern theologians [read: elitists] propound a variety of gods who are unintelligible and inaccessible to the vast majority of humankind?)

I will agree to almost any definition of God which you propose for the simple reason that I deny the existence of any and all of them. I would question what you mean, though, when you say, "worthy of worship." Do you mean that God deserves worship, that He has earned the right to be worshiped? If worship is His due, then why?

Back to Anselm: He is employing circular reasoning. If He did not exist He would not be perfect. He is perfect because He exists!

I stated that the contingency argument falls down because it requires the "ultimate ground" of the universe and assumes a First Cause. By direct implication this denies the possibility of "infinite regress."

Because you cannot conceive that the natural laws of the universe (like little Topsy) were "never born'd but jest grow'd," because you cannot conceive of the grossly improbable occurring, you invent a Deity. The chances of winning the New York State Lottery are about one in twenty-six million, yet someone wins almost every week. Taking into account your mother's and your father's genes, the chances of having the facial features, the voice, the mental and psychological makeup that you do are something of the order of one in several trillion. But you are the you that you are. Again we must distinguish between the improbable and the impossible. What is it that God tells Moses when Moses asks His name? The universe *is*.

Webster's says, "chance—something that happens unpredictably without discernible human intention or observable cause." That pretty much sums up my idea of the universe.

To come back to your last paragraph: If each of the arguments for God has a fallacy, how can the sum of them have truth? What are what you call "the religious experiences of humankind"? Please explain your expression, "worthy of worship."

So long for now.

                    Your friend,

                    Mort

7

Redefinitions or Alternative Conceptions of God in Modern Theology

INTRODUCTORY COMMENT TO ALTERNATIVE CONCEPTS OF GOD

The most likely trump card in the hand of the atheist is the problem of evil. What exactly *is* the problem? It is important to note that the problem arises only with the classical theistic concept of God, namely, God as an omnipotent, perfectly good Being. If your idea of God, for example, is that of an impersonal cosmic force that does not care about our individual destinies, there is no theological problem. (Evil is, of course, always a practical problem but not necessarily a theological problem.)

Consider, then, these three propositions:

1. God is omnipotent (all-powerful).

2. God is perfectly good.

3. Considerable amounts of evil and suffering exist in the world.

Proposition 3 seems to be inconsistent with the first two propositions taken together. If God were all-powerful, He *could* have created a world without evil. And if He were perfectly good, He *would*
have created a world without evil. Yet evils, such as the Holocaust,
exist. Therefore, it appears that God cannot be both all-powerful and
all-good.

The classical theist attempts to rebut the charge of inconsistency
by maintaining that it is possible that an omnipotent, perfectly good
Deity has good enough reason for permitting evil, a reason such as
the fostering of human freedom (the free-will defense) or perhaps a
reason that our finite minds cannot comprehend.

But consider the price the classical theist must pay for the defense
of Divine omnipotence. Imagine a parent who sees his or her child
run into the street in front of a moving vehicle but who refrains from
rescuing the child because he or she has some "deeper reason" not
comprehensible to the rest of us. What would we think of such a
parent? Analogously, a God who could have prevented the Holocaust
but did not intervene for some hidden reason is not the kind of Deity
who inspires worship for most of us. Thus, although it is logically
possible that an omnipotent, perfectly good Deity has a reason for
allowing the Holocaust that we do not understand, it is repugnant to
the moral conscience of most sensitive individuals to think of God as
"hiding His face," being able to intervene but choosing not to do so.

For this reason and other considerations, Jewish thinkers and religious thinkers of other faiths have developed alternative or revisionary
concepts of God. Harold Kushner, for example, has developed a
concept of God as perfectly good but not omnipotent. God, Kushner
asserts, is not a cosmic agent who is responsible for bad things happening to us but rather a perfectly good Being limited in power who
is with us in our suffering but unable to prevent it. "From that per-
spective," Kushner writes, "there ought to be a sense of relief in
coming to the conclusion that God is not doing this to us. If God is
a God of justice and not of power, then He can still be on our

side when bad things happen to us."[1] This view is known as *limited theism.*

Another limited theist was Rabbi Milton Steinberg (1903–1950), spiritual leader of the Park Avenue Synagogue in New York City. Limited theists argue that nature is in the process of evolving, according to God's will, to higher and better levels. But in each species in the universe, there remains some lower level of development. Evil is to be found in these lower stages. Indeed, Kushner quotes Steinberg's theory that evil is "the still unremoved scaffolding of the edifice of God's creativity."[2]

More radical still than the limited theism of Steinberg and Kushner was that of their teacher and, indeed, one of the great minds of twentieth-century Jewish thought, Mordecai M. Kaplan. Mordecai M. Kaplan (1881–1983), professor at the Jewish Theological Seminary and founder of the Reconstructionist movement in Judaism, held that the idea of God had to be reconstructed to fit the modern age. Kaplan's view is known as *religious naturalism.* In this view, God is not a personal Being but rather "*the sum of the animating, organizing forces and relationships which are forever making a cosmos out of chaos,*"[3] experienced by us as the Power that makes for salvation—that impels us to become fully human. God is thus a creative *power* or *process* in the universe that makes for the improvement of human life.

These last two concepts of God are among the positions outlined in a book entitled *Finding God: Ten Jewish Responses,*[4] which the

---

1. Harold Kushner, *When Bad Things Happen to Good People* (New York: Schocken Books, 1981), p. 44.

2. Ibid., p. 55.

3. Mordecai M. Kaplan, *The Meaning of God in Modern Jewish Religion* (New York: Reconstructionist Press, 1962), p. 76.

4. Rifat Sonsino and Daniel B. Syme, *Finding God: Ten Jewish Responses* (New York: Union of American Hebrew Congregations, 1986).

rabbi gave to Mort Shor. Thus, there are alternatives to classical theism in contemporary Jewish thought.

A revisionary concept of God that is popular in Protestant Christian theology, and has been introduced into Jewish theology by Rabbi Kaufman's book *The Case for God,* is *process theology.* Process theology is based on the thought of two eminent philosophers, British-born Alfred North Whitehead[5] (1861–1947), who came to America to teach at Harvard University, and the American thinker Charles Hartshorne[6] (1897–   ). *Process* means an ongoing series of events that leads to novelty. Whitehead's picture of the universe (elaborated in such major works as *Science and the Modern World, Religion in the Making,* and *Process and Reality*) is that of a creative movement to novelty—a creative flow of events. A flower, a tree, a brook, a pond—each of these is a new manifestation of nature, ever evolving and ever renewing itself. But nature is not only novelty. If it were, there would be nothing but chaos. Nature is also order, structure, and harmony. Whitehead thus developed the concept of God as the source of nature's balance between order and novelty.

---

5. Philosopher and mathematician, Alfred North Whitehead was born in 1861 in Ramsgate, Kent, the son of an English pastor. He was educated at Trinity College, Cambridge University, and from 1914 to 1924 he was professor and dean of the faculty at the Imperial College of Science and Technology at the University of London. In 1924 he became professor of philosophy at Harvard University. In collaboration with Bertrand Russell, he wrote the new classic *Principia Mathematica.* Among his many works of philosophy are *Process and Reality, Science and the Modern World, Adventures of Ideas, Symbolism, Modes of Thought, The Aims of Education,* and *Religion in the Making.* These books reflect Whitehead's abiding interest in bringing to bear on modern culture the temperate and judicious findings of philosophic speculation. Alfred North Whitehead died in 1947.

6. Emeritus Professor of philosophy at the University of Texas, Charles Hartshorne (1897–   ) is associated with Whitehead as one of the two major process philosophers. However, he is also an original thinker in his own right. His position is known as *panentheism,* as distinguished from *pan-*

In classical theism, God was conceived of as immutable or unchanging. The uniqueness of process theology is that both Whitehead and Hartshorne develop a *dipolar* concept of a God who in one aspect is unchanging but, in another phase, is ever changing, growing, and in process (hence, *process* theology).

The first aspect of God that Whitehead refers to is God's *primordial nature.* This makes God the unchanging source of all the relevant potentiality and ideals that lure events to novelty and realization. The *process* aspect of God is called the *consequent nature*: the world-process becomes immanent and immortalized in God and woven into God's higher harmony. The point is that considerable freedom for self-actualization is given to God's creatures. God works by *persuasion* rather than by coercion or force. It is up to human beings either to actualize or to reject the Divine ideals. God is, thus, not omnipotent. Human beings are *really* true partners of God. Thus, process theology develops in a novel, contemporary way the Judaic conception of the partnership of God and persons.

This idea is further elaborated by Charles Hartshorne. For Hartshorne, God is the world-mind or world-soul. His view is called *panentheism*. Whereas in pantheism, God is equated with nature or the universe, in panentheism the universe is *in* God. God, for Hartshorne, is the universal cosmic mind or agent who possesses adequate but not total power. In contrast to Einstein, Hartshorne believes that God *does* play dice with the universe. There *is* chance in the universe, but because of God, chance is not all-pervasive because God, the source of order, sets limits to chance. What Hartshorne is saying is that God's plan for the world is indeterminate in its details. The world-

---

theism. Like Whitehead, Hartshorne holds that God is dipolar—having two aspects. One aspect Hartshorne calls the Divine *existence*, that is, God as a necessarily existent Being, who in this aspect of His being is absolute and unchanging. The second aspect is the Divine *actuality*, which is that aspect of God that is constantly growing and is in process within the universe.

process is not an idle duplicate of an eternal plan. There is real novelty and creative process in the world. The idea of omnipotence, for Hartshorne, is a theological mistake. God is the maximal power but does not possess all the power in the universe, for if this were the case, we would be sheer puppets or automata.

Thus, mainly because of the problem of evil and the need to uphold human freedom, some philosophers and theologians reject the idea of God's omnipotence. What we need, therefore, is a concept of God broad enough to encompass limited theism as well as classical theism. We suggest "a unitary actuality that is supremely worthy of worship."

Classical theists hold that only an omnipotent Deity is worthy of worship, because only an omnipotent Deity is truly sovereign of the universe. Limited theists hold that a God who had the power to stop the Holocaust but didn't is not worthy of worship. It's thus a matter of judgment, evaluation, and temperament. The alternatives are classical theism, limited theism, religious naturalism, agnosticism (suspending judgment), or atheism.

Through the correspondence, we hope the reader glimpses an insight, a thought, or an idea that will generate some clarity in reassessing the perennial issue of the nature and existence of God. Many people need a faith for life and some accept unquestioning faith. Others ask: Faith in what? Still others will eschew religious commitment altogether. We hope that this phase of the correspondence sharpens the alternatives and leads to an informed theological choice.

CR CR RD RD

April 11, 1991

Dear Mort,

I saw your sister-in-law Edythe the other day, and she remarked, in a humorous vein, about her concern that my views might really be changed as a result of our correspondence. Should I worry?

It's time that I stated clearly my views. Also, I promised you in my last letter that I would describe some alternative God-concepts or modern theologies.

First, let me state my views and also what I hope to gain by this dialogue with you.

Our subject is the existence and nature of God. Where we differ is: I have faith in the existence of God, that is, I believe in a Higher Power. You do not.

The theological question I am asked the most as a rabbi is: Why did God allow the Holocaust?

If God is omnipotent, I am forced to agree with the premise behind the question: that God *could* have prevented the Holocaust but chose not to do so. Finding this view problematic to my moral conscience, I then proceed to search for alternative theologies such as:

1. The religious naturalism of the contemporary Jewish thinker Mordecai M. Kaplan.[7] Kaplan defines God as

---

7. Mordecai M. Kaplan (1881–1983), author, educator, and founder of the Reconstructionist movement, immigrated from Lithuania to the United States at the age of nine. He studied at City College of New York and

a. the Power that makes for salvation, by which he means the Power that impels man to become fully human, and

b. the creative process—the sum of the animating, organizing forces and relationships which are forever making a cosmos out of chaos.

2. The limited theism of Rabbi Milton Steinberg,[8] a twentieth-century religious leader and thinker who envisaged God as the Mind-Energy of the Universe, but who is self-limited in His power. He held that if man is to have real freedom, God's control cannot be complete.

Columbia University and then entered the rabbinic program of the Jewish Theological Seminary, the center of the Conservative movement. Ordained in 1902, he served briefly as rabbi of an Orthodox congregation in New York, leaving to become dean of the newly founded Teacher's Institute of the Jewish Theological Seminary. He was also a professor of Homiletics and Philosophies of Religion at the Rabbinical School of the Jewish Theological Seminary.

Originally, Kaplan intended Reconstructionism as a liberal wing of the Conservative movement. It is now a fourth movement in Judaism, with Orthodox, Reform, and Conservative Judaism.

The fundamental idea of Reconstructionism is that Judaism must be reconstructed and reinterpreted to fit the needs of the modern Jew. For Kaplan this meant seeing Judaism as the evolving religious civilization of the Jewish people, the traditional commandments as folkways, and God as that power or process within the universe that fosters human growth and creativity. The view of God as power or process within nature is known as *religious naturalism*, in contrast to supernaturalism, in which God is viewed as an omnipotent Supreme Being or spiritual person who created the universe and can intervene in the natural course of events by suspending the laws of nature.

8. Milton Steinberg (1903–1950), Rabbi of the Park Avenue Synagogue in New York, was for a long time a disciple of Mordecai M. Kaplan and

Since it is not clear that Kaplan's idea of God is that of a unitary actuality and since Steinberg's concept was insufficiently developed (he died at forty-six), I found more satisfaction in a contemporary movement called process theology, based on the philosophies of Alfred North Whitehead and Charles Hartshorne, according to whom God is unlimited in some respects, limited in others. I will outline this theology in a subsequent letter.

What I want to learn from our dialogue is whether a stronger case for God can be made holding the plain man's view of the omnipotent God or by seeking a re-definition of God along the lines of Kaplan, Steinberg, process theology, etc. In fact, I have written two manu-scripts articulating The Case for God. Manuscript "A" defends the omnipotent God. Manuscript "B" defends the finite-infinite God of process theology.

I would be glad to show you these manuscripts.

At present, I am not convinced of either position, al-though I do believe in a Higher Power. Thus, at present, I am a *religious* agnostic; on the basis of faith, I believe in God, a Higher Power, but am agnostic about the *nature* of this Power.

Through our dialogue I hope to clarify my views on the *nature* of God.

---

inclined toward Reconstructionism. However, he ultimately parted company with Kaplan's theology, insisting that God must be a conscious Being, a Universal Mind-Energy or Spirit. Nevertheless, he differed from classical theism in holding that God's power was limited by the laws of nature and human freedom.

Edythe's worry is that you might start to chip away at my belief in the *existence* of God. I'll have to take my chances.

Your friend,

Bill

CஜGஜ ௮௮

April 14, 1991

Dear Bill,

In your letter of April 11 you ask if you should worry about your exposure to my infection with the virus of skepticism. That is a tough question. I am tempted to say, "Where ignorance is bliss, 'tis folly to be wise." That sounds awfully smug and downright arrogant. So I won't say it!

One of our problems is that I *do* have the arrogance to believe that I am the possessor of the truth, that God is man's invention. While you say that you believe in the existence of a "Higher Power" I believe that you have the humility to assume that there is a possibility, albeit remote, that you might be mistaken. So, maybe you *should* worry!

The basic problem that you seem to face in formulating your concept of God is the famous problem of evil. If we postulate the plain man's God, the problem disappears. God is omnipotent and His ways are inscrutable. He rewards virtue and punishes evil. He answers our prayers, although not always in ways that are clear and understandable to us. Why does He *seem* to permit evil? Why the Holocaust? Why the African famines? We cannot understand but we know that God is good and He has His reasons.

It is only when we start to think rationally about God, when we try to apply the same standards to Him that we apply to man, when we start to ask logical questions—it is only then that evil becomes a problem. And it is then that the theologians start to cut and trim and tailor their God-concepts. The modern theologians try to find a compromise solution to the great problem of evil by modifying the concept of God. First we learn that God is no longer omnipotent; His powers are limited. Man commits evil despite God. Then the theologians continue changing His image. Our plain man's God loses His personhood. Then He becomes a Power: the Power to create salvation, the Power to bring cosmos out of chaos. Lately He has become a Process.

Then we have the theologians who do not say that God is limited. They say that He is "unlimited in some respects."

It would be interesting to learn what new concepts of God will appear over the next century as totally new problems arise that cannot be explained by today's theology. *Webster's* defines theology as "rational interpretation of religious faith, practice and experience." This strikes me as an oxymoron.

I should be delighted to read your two manuscripts giving "The Case for God" and to send you my profane observations.

I am still puzzled by the question, "Why do you believe in a Higher Power?"

Your friend,

Mort

8

Believing in God:
Reasons for and Against

April 19, 1991

Dear Mort,

In your recent letter, you ask me why I believe in a Higher Power, the reasons for my faith.

The main reason I believe in a Higher Power is the mystery of the mind. How does a three-pound substance—a brain—think, write symphonies, etc.? I came across an article in the *Reader's Digest* by a doctor about near death experiences (NDEs), in which, for example, a person has a heart attack, passes out, and awakens to find himself floating above his body, going through a tunnel, and encountering a Being of light. Needless to say, NDEs are controversial: some say that they are merely psychological; others assert that they are glimpses into the next world.

I do not want to enter into this controversy. What I do wish to emphasize is that the author of this article mentions that in his search for a scientific explanation of NDEs he learned about esoteric experiments conducted by the neurosurgeon Wilder Penfield. When Penfield electrically stimulated an area of the brain called the sylvian fissure, patients frequently had the experience of feeling as if they weren't there, hearing music and reviewing life events. Then the article states that Penfield readily admitted that the energy source that powers the mind is a total mystery: "It is clear that to survive after death, the mind must establish a connection with a source of energy other than the brain. . . . It is not unreasonable to hope that after death the mind may waken to another source of energy."[1]

Moreover, consider the creativity of Mozart, composing symphonies while still a child, or Beethoven, writing symphonies when he was deaf. In a letter, Mozart wrote that he heard the symphony in his head, all the parts "all at once" before actually composing the work. And he referred to this as "the best gift I have my Divine maker to thank for."[2]

Again, writing about Whitehead, Victor Lowe states that Whitehead's rationalism did not permit him to say that novelty just happens. "His religious humility told him whence it came."[3]

---

1. Melvin Morse, M.D., with Paul Perry, "Children of the Light," condensed from *Closer to the Light, Reader's Digest*, March 1991.

2. Brewster Ghiselin, ed., *The Creative Process* (Berkeley, CA: University of California Press, 1952), p. 45.

3. Victor Lowe, *Understanding Whitehead* (Baltimore, MD: Johns Hopkin's Press, 1966), p. 47.

My religious humility leads me to believe that whatever creative things I accomplish are due partly to me and partly to the Higher Power to which I believe my mind is plugged in.[4] This is why I believe in a Higher Power, a Universal Mind I call "God."

How do you account for creativity—especially the astounding creativity of a Mozart?

Look forward to hearing from you.

Your friend,

Bill

൫ ൫ ൬ ൬

April 23, 1991

Dear Bill,

Re yours of April 19: Let us dispense with the near death experiences very quickly. Neither you nor I believe in an afterlife. The hallucinations of someone in a semiconscious or unconscious state do not really have any bearing on our dialogue.

What in the world does the electrical stimulation of certain brain areas (and the reaction thereto) have to do with the existence of a Higher Power? Why in the world should our ignorance of the workings of the brain and the mind lead one to believe in a Higher Power? Why

---

4. I owe the phrase "plugged into a Higher Power" to a theological discussion with a colleague, Cantor Richard A. Wolberg.

should the existence of genius lend credence to the existence of a Higher Power? What is the connection between spectacularly gifted minds and a Higher Power?

How, then, do I account for creativity? How do I account for invention, intelligence, genius, for Mozart, for Michelangelo, for Shakespeare? I do not do what the ancients did when they could not account for lightning and thunder, for floods and storms. I do not attribute to a Higher Power those phenomena which I cannot explain today. Perhaps I will be able to explain them tomorrow.

By the way, quoting Victor Lowe on Whitehead is simply quoting the Bible to prove religion.

You state that your religious humility leads you to believe that a Higher Power is responsible, in part, for whatever creative things you accomplish. You do not, however, support or explain this belief. Why do you believe that? Why are you not solely responsible for your creativity? Would you say that this Higher Power is also responsible for any of the destructive things that you do? I assume that your reply to this is in the negative. Why the dichotomy? Why can you not assume full responsibility for the positive and negative things that you think and do?

I look forward with real pleasure to your answers to all of my questions. (Who said, "A fool can ask more questions than a wise man can answer."?)

Your friend,

Mort

P.S. Frankly, Bill, I do not have a particularly high regard for the *Reader's Digest* as a source.

9

Reaction to the Book
Finding God:
Ten Jewish Responses

Dear Bill,

I have been reading the book you lent me, *Finding God: Ten Jewish Responses* by Sonsino and Syme,[1] and am really enjoying it.

I will not attempt to address the first seven chapters. These cover the biblical, rabbinical, mystic, and supernatural interpretations of God. I do not think that you and I differ very much in our approach to these.

Chapter 8, "The Limited Theism of Steinberg," deals with the ideas and beliefs of Rabbi Milton Steinberg (1903–1950). At the outset, Steinberg states that we must accept the existence of God on faith alone. In his *Anatomy of Faith* he states, "For like other propositions, that of the exis-

---

1. Rifat Sonsino and Daniel B. Syme, *Finding God: Ten Jewish Responses* (New York: Union of American Hebrew Congregations, 1986).

tence of God is not completely provable. It remains the conclusion of an act of faith."[2] In a very real sense, this could be the end of our dialogue. Faith, by its very nature, not only does not require proof but is antithetical to proof. If something can be proved, faith is not only not required but is a contradiction. (Incidentally, what does Rabbi Steinberg mean by God not being "completely" provable?)

In *A Believing Jew*, he attempts to "prove" God's existence by employing the argument that the creation of our universe required a Supreme Being. He says, "Here before me unfolds a universe which is dynamic, creative and rational in the sense that everything in it conforms to the law of its own being, a world that has produced in living things what seems to be purposiveness and in man the phenomenon of consciousness. No other theory except that which posits a Thought-Will as the essence of things fits such a scene."[3]

First, I am sure that Rabbi Steinberg knew of other theories that fit such a scene. That aside, however, this is, of course, the oft-repeated argument that since I cannot conceive of such a miraculously ordered universe just happening, then God must have created it. An obvious *non sequitur*. My mind is obviously inadequate to imagine the formation of the universe. It must follow, then, that a superior mind must have dreamed up (created) the universe.

In common with so many theologians, Rabbi Steinberg gives God qualities, attributes, characteristics: "God is

---

2. Milton Steinberg, *Anatomy of Faith*, ed. Arthur A. Cohen (New York: Harcourt, Brace Jovanovich, 1960), p. 74.

3. Milton Steinberg, *A Believing Jew* (New York: Harcourt, Brace Jovanovich, 1951), p. 21.

Absolute in the sense of being a Creator. . . . God is limited in his powers. . . . God is indubitably the power of rationality, of design, of order. . . ."[4] How does Steinberg know God's traits?

In attempting to explain how evil can coexist with God, the obvious is evaded. If we do not postulate God, we have no need to find explanations for evil. Every theologian seems to find another explanation for the God/evil problem and each explanation seems more strained than the other. Steinberg explains it by stating that God's powers are limited. In effect he says, "God is great. Look at the wonderful universe he has created. Evil? We-e-e-l, perhaps God isn't so great. Perhaps he is limited and cannot do anything about evil." He says, "The concept of irrational evil prevents us from ascribing to God that which probably [sic] should not be ascribed to Him. God is exempted, not from the struggle, but from the responsibility for the elements of chance within His universe."[5]

What does he mean by "probably" and why is God let off the hook and allowed to go scot-free for the evil in His world?

In my next letter I will be dealing with Rabbi Mordecai M. Kaplan, one of my favorite theologians, who I seriously believe was a closet atheist—or at least a closet agnostic.

All the best to you and your family.

Your friend,

Mort

---

4. Steinberg, *Anatomy of Faith*, pp. 273–274.
5. Steinberg, *Anatomy of Faith*, p. 275.

April 11, 1991

Dear Bill,

The chapter on Rabbi Mordecai M. Kaplan in *Finding God* is for me the most fascinating. The first quotation, in effect, spills the beans.

> The conditions that enabled Judaism to flourish in the past are irrevocably gone with the wind. Nothing less than original and creative thinking in terms of present day realities and future responsibilities can create anew the conditions which are indispensable for Jewish survival.[6]

Here, Dr. Kaplan tells us that the supernatural, anthropomorphic God—the One who rewarded virtue and punished evil, the One who answered prayers and performed miracles—no longer exists. He was, however, a very important God. He enabled the Jewish people to endure over the millennia while other mightier peoples arose and disappeared. Now that this old God is gone, Rabbi Kaplan tells us that we must have a new One, one suitable to "present day realities" (read: the scientific age) who will "create anew the conditions [for] Jewish survival."

Before going into the basic raw materials out of which Dr. Kaplan fashions his new God, I want to refer to Kaplan's view (which I share completely) that Judaism is not just a religion. It is, in contrast with Christianity but simi-

---

6. From the *Reconstructionist* 8, 1942. Quoted in Sonsino and Syme, *Finding God*, p. 107.

lar to Arabism, a civilization. It comprises a religion, a history, a culture, a literature, customs, etc. For Judaism to survive, Kaplan states Jews must partake fully in their "civilization," that is, in *all* aspects of it. But how can they participate in the religion if the old God is dead? Simple. Let's make a new One. We follow Voltaire's observation that "If God did not exist, it would be necessary to invent Him."

So Dr. Kaplan invents a brand-new twentieth-century Deity. He is not supernatural. He is the God of goodness, virtue, order, and all good and positive things in the universe. In fact, in Kaplan's words, God is:

> "The sum of everything in the world that renders life significant and worthwhile—or holy.
>
> The totality of those forces in life that render human life worthwhile. The Power that impels man to become fully human.
>
> The sum of the animating, organizing forces and relationships which are forever making a cosmos out of chaos.
>
> The Power that makes for the fulfillment of all valid ideals."[7]

In brief:

God is the power that makes for salvation.

---

7. Mordecai M. Kaplan, *The Meaning of God in Modern Jewish Religion* (New York: Reconstructionist Press, 1962), p. 76. See also Kaplan's *Judaism Without Supernaturalism* (New York: Reconstructionist Press, 1958), pp. 114–115.

Isn't our friend Rabbi Kaplan taking morality, ethics, virtue, goodness, etc., and simply relabeling them God? Regarding Kaplan's view of evil, the authors Sonsino and Syme state, ". . . evil is that part of the universe that God has not as yet subdued."[8] And Kaplan himself says, "[It is] chaos still uninvaded by creative energy, sheer chance unconquered by will and intelligence."[9]

"God has not as yet subdued."[10] ". . . uninvaded by creative energy . . ."[11] Aren't we coming very close to our old anthropomorphic God?

Regarding belief in God, Kaplan says, "To believe in God means to take for granted that it is man's destiny to rise above the brute and to eliminate all forms of violence and exploitation from our society."[12]

Sonsino and Syme go on to say, "If God is, as Kaplan argued, the Power which makes for truth, for good, for justice, for freedom, then whenever we display moral responsibility we manifest the presence of God. To the extent that we strive to know the moral law and live up to it, we achieve, in Kaplan's words, 'Salvation' or 'self-realization.'"[13]

Bill, I strongly believe in truth, justice, freedom, the elimination of all forms of violence, etc. That simply means that I am a moral man. What does that have to do with the concept "God"? It seems that Kaplan has substituted

8. Sonsino and Syme, *Finding God*, p. 116.

9. Kaplan, *The Meaning of God*, pp. 72–73.

10. Sonsino and Syme, *Finding God*, p. 116.

11. Kaplan, *The Meaning of God*, p. 72.

12. Kaplan, *Without Supernaturalism*, p. 112.

13. Sonsino and Syme, *Finding God*, p. 112.

the word *God* for the word *ethics* or *morality* and claims that he has discovered or invented a God for the modern man.

When he writes about prayer, it seems to me that he is on even weaker ground. What meaning can there possibly be in the prayer the man utters, "Hear O Israel the Lord our God the Lord is one" or "Blessed art Thou King of the universe . . . ," especially when uttered in an ancient language which he does not understand. He reads a standardized prayer from a prayer book. He might just as well read a geometric proof from a mathematics book for all the meaning it has for him. Correction: It has one meaning for him. He is participating in one aspect of Jewish civilization, *not* that of religion but that of tradition.

To sum up, Bill, it seems that Kaplan awoke to the fact that "the God of our fathers" is a fiction, but fiction or fact, He sustained the Jewish people for thousands of years. He believed that for Judaism to continue it must have a God and voilà! he invented a new one for us.

Why do I call Rabbi Kaplan a closet atheist? He did not convince me that there is a God and I am sure that he was much smarter than I am, so I assume that he did not convince himself either.

Let me hear from you.

> With very warmest regards.
>
> Your friend,
>
> Mort

April 16, 1991

Dear Bill,

This is a continuation of my comments on *Finding God* by Sonsino and Syme.

In trying to deal with our old friend the problem of evil, Erich Fromm[14] has arrived at what I feel is the ultimate evasion of the question, "Is there a God?" or "What is the Nature of God?" It is the old business of God is Nature; God is Love; God is Virtue. But let me get to some of the actual writings. The authors (Sonsino and Syme) state, "According to Fromm, religion is a fundamental human need. In fact, he derives his definition of religion from the list of our basic personal necessities."[15] They then quote Fromm: "I understand by religion any system of thought and action shared by a group which gives the individual a frame of orientation and an object of devotion."[16]

---

14. One of the Jewish responses outlined in *Finding God*. Erich Fromm (1900–1980) was a renowned Jewish humanist and psychoanalyst. Unlike Kaplan, who believed that God is an actual cosmic power or process within nature that works through human beings, Fromm held that God is not at all a power over or beyond us but rather is a symbol of humanity's highest value and most desirable good. This is precisely what is meant by *religious humanism*; the word *God* is used as a symbol for the best in man. By contrast, the secular humanist refuses to use the word *God* even as a symbol and simply believes that humanity can thus either be agnostic or atheistic. *Agnosticism* is the view that we simply know nothing about God and therefore must suspend judgment about whether or not a Deity exists. *Atheism*, by contrast, is the explicit denial or negation of Divine existence.

15. Sonsino and Syme, *Finding God*, p. 120.

16. From *Psychoanalysis and Religion*, quoted in *Finding God*, p. 120.

The authors then go on to say "There is no individual, or culture, which does not have a religious need; that is, a frame of orientation and an object of devotion."[17] We all look at the world from a particular vantage point and cherish certain high ideals. However, this tells us very little about the contents of our needs. A person may worship animals, trees, idols, money, leaders. In fact, "If we scratch the surface of modern man we discover any number of individualized primitive forms of religion."[18]

I am an individual who does not have a religious need or an object of devotion. And do we all cherish high ideals? How about Attila the Hun, Adolf Hitler, Stalin, the local drug pusher?

In tracing the development of the God-concept from our plain man's God to Erich Fromm's God, we come to the point where "God is . . . not a reality in itself."[19]

So what does Fromm leave us with? Be a good little boy. Be virtuous; be kind; strive to improve mankind. All worthy goals, but what have they to do with the concept of God?

O.K., Bill, you tell me!

Love to Nathalie and the kids . . .

Your friend,

Mort

---

17. Ibid., pp. 120–121.

18. Ibid., p. 29.

19. Erich Fromm, *You Shall Be as Gods: A Radical Interpretation of the Old Testament and Its Traditions* (New York: Henry Holt & Co., 1991), p. 18.

April 16, 1991

Dear Mort,

I wrote you three letters last week, so you should have received them by now. I have just received your letter about the theology of Mordecai M. Kaplan, the great twentieth-century Jewish philosopher, founder of Reconstructionist Judaism, and author of many books including *Judaism as a Civilization*, *The Meaning of God in Modern Jewish Religion*, and *The Future of the American Jew*.

You are quite right that his aim was to reconstruct Jewish theology and ideology to fit modern scientific thought. However, you don't have his theology quite right. You make the same mistake most people make—interpreting him as a humanist who simply equates "God" with ethical values.

In his book *The Meaning of God in Modern Jewish Religion*, he explicitly states that humanism is not enough. In addition to believing in the importance of living an ethical life, as the humanist does, Kaplan goes beyond humanism in holding that the universe is so constituted as to enable human beings to achieve salvation (i.e., the self-fulfillment that derives from the ethical life). This is what he means by God as the Power that makes for salvation, namely, "God" refers to the salvation-making process in the cosmos that impels and endorses our quest for the maximum life.

His argument is as follows: "*Just as the will to live testifies (in an intuitive, not in a logical sense) to the reality of life, the will to live the maximum life testifies to the realizable character of such life.*"[20]

Belief in God, Kaplan states, is *"belief in the existence of a Power conducive to salvation which is the fulfillment of human destiny"*[21] (which is therefore more than humanism). He holds that God is not a Being but a process or power transcending us which is therefore more than humanism. He writes that God, "the Power transcending ourselves, that makes for salvation, also inheres in all the forces of our minds and wills."[22] Thus, for Kaplan, God is both transcendent and immanent.

The question raised by Kaplan's theology is whether or not there is such a salvation-making process in the universe or whether the universe is devoid of meaning apart from human beings.

Is the human being the only source of meaning for you? Is the universe, apart from us, "a tale told by an idiot, full of sound and fury, signifying nothing," as Shakespeare wrote in *Macbeth*?

If you deny Kaplan's claim that the universe is inherently meaningful vis-à-vis human beings, what are you left with?

I look forward to your response.

Your friend,

Bill

---

20. Kaplan, *The Meaning of God*, p. 328.

21. Mordecai M. Kaplan, *The Future of the American Jew* (New York: Reconstructionist Press, 1967), p. 172.

22. Ibid., p. 183.

April 18, 1991

Dear Bill,

Re yours of April 16 defending the theology of Rabbi Mordecai M. Kaplan, let us not forget that he *was* a rabbi. As such, he could not very well simply equate God with ethical values in so many words. That would be tantamount to atheism. That is, however, what his theology boils down to.

How can one have a theology without the lead actor, God? So he did what all theologians do. He claimed attributes for his God and for his God's universe with no basis for his claims other than his unsupported statements. For example:

1. The universe is so constructed as to enable human beings to achieve salvation. (How does he know this?)

2. God is the power transcending ourselves that makes for salvation and also inheres in all the forces of our minds and wills. (How does Kaplan know this?)

3. "God" refers to the salvation-making process in the cosmos that implies and endorses man's quest for the maximum life. (That's quite a definition but also purely Kaplan's invention.)

4. Salvation . . . is the fulfillment of human destiny. (It is not the fulfillment of my destiny.)

All of the above, and much more, are very high-sounding statements all made of whole cloth. Rabbi Kaplan makes the statements without the slightest shred of evidence to support them. How does he know all this about God? Obviously, he has invented his God.

A favorite word of theologians is *transcendence* in its many forms. To quote, "'Transcendence' is an extremely ambiguous term."[23]

You put his argument as follows: *"Just as the will to live testifies (in an intuitive, not in a logical sense) to the reality of life, the will to live the maximum life testifies to the realizable character of such a life."* A few questions:

1. What is the meaning of the term *reality of life*?

2. What is the "realizable character" of such life?

3. All animals exhibit a will to live. Does Dr. Kaplan's statement apply to all animals?

We (you and I) are constantly using the word *meaning*—the meaning of life, the meaning of the universe, the meaning of salvation, etc. I don't believe that I really know what you mean by "meaning." And I am not entirely certain that I know what I mean. When I try to think of what gives meaning to my life, I automatically think of my family and one or two close friends, about how I feel about them, about my relationship with them. That is what gives meaning to my life. Perhaps it is too narrow a view. What gives meaning to your life? As for the meaning of the universe, it *is* a tale told by an idiot. And

---

23. William E. Kaufman, *Contemporary Jewish Philosophies* (New York: Reconstructionist Press, 1976).

in such a universe, we are left with those values that man has adopted as "good" (only because he has found over the millennia that they are practical). As a matter of fact, the order of importance of values (not to steal, not to lie, not to kill, etc.) varies from culture to culture. The Japanese concept of the *on*, a word almost untranslatable but vaguely similar to *obligation*, stands at the top of all ethical forces. It is nonexistent in the West.

So what am I left with in this meaningless universe? I am left with the meaningfulness of Sylvia, my sister, my friends Melvin and Eduardo, and even you!

Your friend,

Mort

10

Process Theology

April 15, 1991

Dear Mort,

In my previous letter to you, I mentioned a contemporary movement called process theology, based on the philosophies of Alfred North Whitehead and Charles Hartshorne.

Essentially, Whiteheadian process theology is a revolt against the plain man's concept of God as an omnipotent, immutable or unchanging, controlling power who determines our destiny through the use of coercive power. Against this, the process thinkers conceive of God's power in a different way. They say that God works by *persuasive* rather than *coercive* power. What does this mean?

Process is the realization of possibilities and potentialities. The nature of God is dipolar—having two aspects. The primordial nature contains all the possibilities, all the pure potentials. Whitehead calls these potentials eternal objects. I call the primordial nature the pattern of all possibilities. Through His primordial nature, God provides each worldly actuality with its initial aim toward its self-realization, a lure toward the ideal, toward the good. But each worldly actuality is *free* to refuse the lure. This is why there is evil in the world. (Thus, God cannot be blamed for evil, which accounts in part for the appeal of process theology.)

The other aspect of God is His *consequent* nature. Unlike the traditional God who is immutable, the process God is *in process* with the universe (another reason it is called process theology). That is, what happens in the world is synthesized in the Divine memory. Thus, God *grows* and develops in process with the world. I call the consequent nature of God the synthesis of all actualities. Thus, God is the pattern of all possibilities and the synthesis of all actualities.

Now, what's the evidence for all this? For process theology, God is the ground of order, novelty, and value.

If each element in the universe contributed equally to it, there would be chaos. Only if there is a preeminent ordering entity (arranging the possibilities and presenting them in graded fashion to the actualities) can we account for the order in the universe.

There is novelty in the universe. Why not just sameness? Because, according to process theology, of God's creative lure to each creature's self-realization.

Finally, without God, there are no eternal values. Dead is dead. God acts to conserve our values in His eternal memory.

I like process theology. It is aesthetically rich. The problem with it is that whereas in His primordial nature God is unlimited, in His consequent nature He is limited by what happens in the universe. The advantage here is that God could *not* have prevented the Holocaust. But He also could not unilaterally have caused the Exodus from Egypt or created the universe *ex nihilo* (out of nothing).

I would therefore modify process theology as follows: a Jewish process theology based on Lurianic mysticism or Kabbalah.

Before creation, God was omnipotent. Most of the creation was good. But creation is also tragic. Evil is a by-product of what went wrong in creation. *After* creation, God is limited by the laws of nature, by human freedom, etc. (whether self-limited or limited by the nature of what He created).

That's the best I can do theologically. I think process theology is the best we have to date, but it would be presumptuous to think that it is the truth. It is, I think, the best the human mind can come up with theologically so far, but the universe is so vast and so strange that I would temper my enthusiasm for process theology with some religious agnosticism.

I look forward to your attempt to tear process theology apart bit by bit, but with what scheme of ideas, with what worldview, with what explanation will you replace it? It's easy to be destructive, harder to be constructive.

If you *had* to choose between the plain man's omnipotent God and the process God, which would you choose? Why?

With warmest wishes to Sylvia.

                    Your friend,

                    Bill

            ෬ ෬ ෮ ෮

                                    April 16, 1991

Dear Bill,

In taking up process theology in yours of April 15 you make a number of statements about the nature of God. You say (and these are your quotations):

   1. God works by *persuasive* rather than *coercive* power.

   2. God provides each worldly actuality with its initial aim toward its self-realization, a lure toward the ideal, toward the good.

   3. The process God is *in process* with the universe. . . .

   4. Thus, God *grows* and develops, in process with the world.

   5. There is novelty in the universe. Why not just sameness? Because, according to process theology, of God's lure to each creature's self-realization.

   6. Without God, there are no eternal values. Dead is dead. God acts to conserve our values in His eternal memory.

Bill, how do you know all of these wonderful characteristics of God? How do you know that He (She or It) is persuasive rather than coercive?; that He grows and develops in process with the world?; that He lures the good?; that He has a Divine memory? an eternal memory? How do you know all of the attributes you give Him? (By the way, what is a "worldly actuality"? And would you please translate statement 2 above into simple language so that even I will understand.)

To me, process theology is simply the latest attempt to solve the dilemma posed by the problem of evil. How do we reconcile God and evil? Process theology is as unconvincing as all of the theologies that precede it. It just won't wash. As a matter of fact, 1,736,221 angels can't dance on the head of a pin!

I object to your characterizing my rejection of process theology as destructive. To refuse to accept a fiction as a fact is not destructive. Au contraire!

I really don't know what explanation or "worldview" you are asking me for. When the little green man from outer space arrived on Earth he was puzzled by hearing the word *God*, which did not exist in his language. "What is God?" he asked. "What leads you to believe that He (She or It) really exists? Oh, I see. Your father told you so; and his father told him; and . . . Oh, I see." And as he turned to leave with his seven-legged dog in tow, he remarked, "Isn't it wonderful that conditions on Earth are such that life could develop. Isn't it wonderful that the universe is!"

And on that note I take my leave for now.

Love to all,

Your friend,

Mort

11

Trying Out the
Atheist's Position

April 25, 1991

Dear Mort,

Just for the sake of argument, let me today take the side
of the atheist and see how far I can go with it.

I am angry because my parents died at such young ages—
my mother at fifty-two, my father at sixty-two. The sense-
less evil in the world, both natural (through disease, etc.)
and human (Hitler, etc.), counts against the existence
of an omnipotent and perfectly good God. The world is
simply not good enough to warrant an omnipotent,
good Deity!

To sidestep this problem by positing a Deity supremely
good but limited is silly. Who needs such an incompe-
tent, bungling Deity?

Why then do I not become an atheist? Because there is one question I cannot answer, namely, *Why is there something rather than nothing?*

The atheist's answer to this is: I don't know. But that is *agnosticism*! How can you possibly *know* that there is no Higher Power of any kind?

Agnosticism makes more sense than atheism. There is also *religious agnosticism*, belief in a Higher Power but no claim of knowledge about its nature.

Atheism to me is as problematic (in terms of what we can know) as classical theism. And isn't the atheist angry that life is "a tale told by an idiot?"

You ask me how theologians like Kaplan and Whitehead claim to know. I ask you: How does the atheist know?

Love to Sylvia.

Your friend,

Bill

ଓ ଓ ଓ ଓ

April 16, 1991

Dear Bill,

I don't think that you present an accurate picture of the "side of the atheist." In your letter you become an atheist because you cannot reconcile God with our old friend "the problem of evil." You reject God after having at one time accepted Him. The atheist says that there is no God to reject. Your approach is an emotional (as opposed to rational) one. God did me wrong so I banish Him. The atheist's approach is strictly based on the facts. What God? Where God? Why God?

You ask how can I possibly *know* that there is not a Higher Power of any kind. (I prefer to capitalize Higher Power because we both really mean "Deity" by that term.) I do not *know* that there is no Higher Power any more than I *know* that there is no seven-legged dog. When some form of *independently verifiable* evidence is presented to me, however, indicating (not necessarily proving) the existence of a Higher Power (or of a seven-legged dog), I will begin to have doubts and then may become an agnostic. When that evidence *proves* the existence of a Higher Power, I will become a believer.

In short, the atheist doesn't claim to know that there is no Higher Power. He simply states that since there is no evidence to prove that there is, he must assume that there is not—just as in the case of our proverbial seven-legged dog.

You ask if the atheist is angry that "life is a tale told by an idiot." One must be angry at something or someone. Anger necessitates a target. Can I or should I be angry when it rains on my picnic? How can I be, when there is nothing to be angry at? The believer has the advantage of being angry at an unjust God who ignored his plans for his picnic.

By now you must know that one of my favorite reference books is *Webster's Seventh New Collegiate Dictionary*. My old friend *Webster's* says: "Agnostic—of or relating to the belief that the existence of any ultimate reality (as God) is unknown and probably unknowable." You call yourself a "religious agnostic"? Is that in *Webster's* sense of the word?

Yes, I ask how the theologian can claim to know so much about the nature and attributes of God—and I get no answer to my question. I do not claim to know that God doesn't exist. I claim that I know of no reason (in every sense of the word *reason*) to believe that He does exist.

Why?

All the best to Nathalie and the kids.

Your friend,

Mort

12

The Atheist's Belief System and View of "Spirituality"

April 23, 1991

Dear Mort,

I just read in the *New Republic* an essay on the death of the British political philosopher Michael Oakeshott. The author of the essay quotes an interesting sentence from one of Oakeshott's essays: "Friends are not concerned with what can be made of one another, but only with the enjoyment of one another; and the condition of enjoyment is a ready acceptance of what is and the absence of any desire to change or improve."[1]

I must confess that I found your letter of April 18 delightful, even though it is profoundly atheistic. It's refreshing to find someone like yourself who really believes and is not afraid to say that "life is a tale told by an idiot."

---

1. *New Republic*, May 6, 1991.

You are quite right to question how philosophers and theologians like Whitehead and Kaplan can claim to know so much about God.

Look, I would be the first to admit that maybe you are right; perhaps there is no meaning apart from man. You are also quite right that to define Fromm's humanism as religious is stretching the meaning of "God" too much. At the very least, God must be a unitary actuality (external to us and not only internal within us) that is worthy of worship.

However, you make your claim of nihilism ("life is a tale told by an idiot") dogmatically. How do you *know* there is no meaning in the universe other than human meaning? Since religion is such a pervasive element of human culture, wouldn't it be odd to find that there is nothing to it and those who believe in it are just plain stupid or credulous?

Moreover, how can you simply dismiss faith, religion, and experience—from Moses at the Burning Bush to Rudolf Otto's *Idea of the Holy* and William James' *Varieties of Religious Experience?* In addition to the book *Finding God: Ten Jewish Responses*, I also gave you John Hick's *Philosophy of Religion.* You will note that he thinks that religious experience provides another link in the theistic argument. Could all religious experiences be a product of delusion? Or is it your view that modern man has simply outgrown the need for religion?

I, too, feel sometimes that "life is a tale told by an idiot." I would not be human if I didn't have doubts. But when I consider all the evidence, it seems to be that the order, beauty, and harmony of the universe together with the religious experiences of humankind point to a Being, dimension, process, or Universal Mind in the universe greater than the human. These considerations lead me to doubt my doubts.

Don't you ever doubt your doubts? I feel that I *allow* for the possibility that the atheist might be *right*. I don't feel that you allow for the possibility that the theist might be right.

I look forward to hearing from you.

Love to Sylvia.

Your friend,

Bill

ℭ ℭ ℬ ℬ

April 26, 1991

Dear Mort,

I still am not clear about your belief system.

Robert Coles, the child psychiatrist, author of *The Spiritual Life of Children*, was interviewed in the *Harvard Alumni Gazette*, March 1991. He was asked: "From a psychiatric viewpoint, do you think having a sense of spirituality or religion or religiousness contributes to a child's health?" He answered:

> We all have some sense of spirituality or religiousness even if we are agnostics or atheists and deny an explicit or even implicit interest in conventional dogma as it's

handed down by the various religious groups. I go back to those questions, for instance, that Gauguin asked when he painted that triptych of his in 1897 that hangs in the Boston Museum of Fine Arts. He titled it, "Where do we come from? What are we? Where are we going?" To my mind, that's what spirituality is. It's the capacity for awareness that we all have and the capacity through language to ask these important existential questions. In that sense I think that every one of us has a religious or spiritual side.

Do you agree? Do you see yourself as having a religious or spiritual side—wondering and musing about ultimate questions? How do you respond to the questions: Where do we come from? What are we? Where are we going? Perhaps your answer will clarify to me what your worldview is.

The other day, a week ago Sunday, I was giving a sermon at an interfaith service in a church. In the middle of my sermon, one of my congregants died of a heart attack (he was eighty). You could interpret this as a random occurrence or see some significance of his dying in a House of God.

Everything depends on one's worldview. Do you see reality simply as matter and energy in motion and our human life as a mere random collection of atoms? Is this where we come from?

I look forward to your response.

Love to Sylvia.

Your friend,

Bill

April 29, 1991

Dear Bill,

One of the basic problems with our dialogue is that you use terminology which can have a variety of meanings and I frequently do not know what meaning you mean to convey. A prime example was cited in my letter of April 18. You talk about "meaning"—the meaning of life, the meaning of the universe—and I don't know what you are trying to say. Again, in your letter of April 26, you ask about my "belief system." What is a belief system? Or better yet, what do *you* mean by a belief system?

You quote Dr. Coles as saying that "we all have some sense of spirituality or religiousness even if we are agnostics or atheists. . . ." Without knowing what Dr. Coles means by these two terms, I cannot agree or disagree. If he accepts *Webster's* definitions of religion and religious I must take issue with him. My old friend says: religion— the service or worship of God or the supernatural; and religious—relating or devoted to the divine or that which is held to be of ultimate importance. By these definitions, his statement does not make sense to me.

"Spiritual"—that is quite another matter. If one has an ap- preciation of beauty, if one lives his life by a high code of morality, if one loves and can be loved—then I would say that he has a spiritual side, and in that sense, I too have a spiritual side. But what has that got to do with God? And I too sometimes "wonder and muse" on what I con- sider "ultimate questions." But I do not consider belief in the supernatural or in any other kind of God as an ultimate question. I do not question where we came from because I believe that we came from the primordial ooze. I do not know what you mean by the question, "What are we?" (Again, what do you mean?) And where we are going is so complete a mystery that to muse on it seems to me to be completely pointless.

What in the world is the significance of a man dying in a "House of God"? If a man died in a house of prostitution would you attach some special significance to that? Have you deserted your process God for Yahweh?

Again, what do you mean when you say that everything depends on one's worldview? Reality (in *my* sense of the word) is made up of matter and energy but also ideas, feelings, emotions, personal interactions, and I don't know what else. But I will not assume something else without seeing independently verifiable evidence of the something else.

No, Bill, human life is not "a mere random collection of atoms," as you put it. It is a well-ordered collection of atoms. And where we come from is, as I said, the primordial slime. Or am I again missing your meaning? Maybe you accept the theory about the origin of life and the evolution from the simplest form to man but mean something quite different by your question.

My final question, Bill, is: Are you going to answer all of my questions?

Love to Nathalie.

Your friend,

Mort

P.S. I should like to use a few abbreviations for terms which I use frequently. IVE is independently verifiable evidence. HP is Higher Power. And if I find other terms I use frequently, I will suggest further shortcuts.

13

A Number of Questions—
Including Belief in a
Larger Meaning

April 25, 1991

Dear Bill,

I have asked a number of questions in my letters which you have not answered. Are you avoiding or evading?

1. What do you mean by "reality of life"?

2. What is the "realizable character of such life"?

3. In Dr. Kaplan's argument referring to "the will to live," he ignores the fact that all animals have a will to live. Do Dr. Kaplan's remarks in this connection refer to all animals?

4. What gives meaning to *your* life?

5. How do the theologians know so much about God's attributes?

6. Why is God "worthy of worship"? Does he "deserve" worship?

7. What do *you* mean by "transcend"?

There are many more questions which you have dodged, but I will get to them in later letters.

You ask how I *know* that there is not meaning in the universe other than the human meaning. (We have yet to agree on the meaning of "meaning.") How do I know that there is no seven-legged dog? Until the existence of either of these is proven to me, I must assume that neither of them exists.

As far as the pervasiveness of religion in human culture is concerned, you can give the atheist's explanation of this as well as (or perhaps better than) I can. Yes, I believe that believers are either hungry for belief (see my letter of March 26), brainwashed, or just plain credulous. I do not think that stupidity or intelligence has any bearing on the question. There are people of intelligence on both sides of the issue.

I do not dismiss "religious experience." I class all of it with "Moses at the Burning Bush." It is frequently fascinating mythology. I do not dismiss the stories of Jupiter, Hera, and Mercury, of Wotan and Erda and Siegfried. But I do not accept them as "evidence" of anything.

Again referring to my March 26 letter: Unfortunately, man has not outgrown his need for religion. Perhaps instead of the word *need* I should say "dependence." Unfortunately, the crippled need crutches.

In your letter you say, "When I consider all the evidence. . . ." *Webster's* gives several definitions for the word *evi-*

dence. One of them is, "something that furnishes proof." By that definition, I state unequivocally that you cannot offer a shred of evidence for the existence of a Higher Power.

Do you allow for the possibility that on some remote island which has never been seen by man that a seven-legged dog exists? I do not allow for the possibility that $2 + 2 = 5$ or that the sun will seem to rise in the West tomorrow morning. I will allow for any possibility that is reasonable and makes sense, that is not supported by a lot of mumbo jumbo that is meaningful only to a select "in" group, that doesn't start with false assumptions and attempt to arrive at a sound conclusion. If a theist will give me a reasonable basis for having doubts about my position, then I will say, "Maybe." Nothing that I have heard or read, however, leads me to believe that there is even the remotest possibility that there is a Higher Power. In fact, the theorizing of the theologians reminds me of nothing more than the medieval discussions of how many angels can dance on the head of a pin. The theologians seem to be talking to each other in an esoteric language that I am not sure even they understand.

And, having said that mouthful, I pass the ball to you.

Your friend,

Mort

May 3, 1991

Dear Mort,

I was very much impressed with the article you sent me concerning the lecture by the social critic Christopher Lasch, "The Soul of Man Under Secularism." After reading the article, it seems to me that you share the eighteenth-century Enlightenment's elation that religion was giving way to critical reason. However, unlike Freud, Weber, and Jung, you have not been chilled by what Max Weber described as "the disenchantment of the world," a phrase describing the two-edged scientific progress that enhanced control over nature but destroyed belief in *any larger meaning.*

Here is the crucial difference between the atheist and the believer, or even the seeker. The believer maintains that there is a larger meaning, the seeker searches for a larger meaning.

The atheist, like yourself, asks: What is the meaning of meaning? What is a belief system? You are only interested in, as you say, that which is proven by independently verifiable evidence. (What do you mean by independently?)

To answer your questions: By meaning, I mean "a larger meaning," a conceptual framework which gives cosmic significance to human existence—for example, the idea of Judaism and process theology that man and God are partners in creation, that God created the world unfinished and our purpose is to complete God's work through our creativity. Of course, this is not empirically verifiable. It is what Joseph Campbell calls a myth—a story we tell ourselves to put our life into a framework. Every civilization has myths, showing the human need for cosmic meaning. Religion is more like art than like science. How do you independently verify that Beethoven or Michelangelo was a genius?

What gives meaning to my life is the search, the quest for larger meaning which I am describing.

By the human will to live, Kaplan means the will to live a maximum life, fulfilling our potential, whereas animals live purely by instinct.

Some theologians do not claim to know much about God's attributes. Maimonides,[1] for example, believed only in negative attributes—we can only know what God is not. He was a religious agnostic, the position which I start from as well. (Chapter 4 in *Finding God* deals with Maimonides.) However, unlike Maimonides, I am not satisfied with religious agnosticism and am seeking illumination in systems such as process theology.

It is extremely difficult, because of the problem of evil, to develop an idea of a Deity that is worthy of worship— that deserves our worship. I am trying to discover, formulate, and articulate just such an idea. Theology represents man's effort to transcend (go beyond) his own limitations.

Where theologians differ is on the degree to which this can be done.

---

1. Moses Maimonides (1135–1204), the most famous of the Jewish medieval philosophers, author of *The Guide to the Perplexed*.

Maimonides held that our limitations are such that we cannot know God's positive attributes, only His negative attributes and His manifestations in ethical values such as truth, goodness, justice, etc. Other thinkers, such as Whitehead and Hartshorne, claim that, through reason, we can transcend ourselves and know God as the pattern of all possibility and the synthesis of all actuality. Their belief is in the axiom of intelligibility—that the universe makes sense and that the idea of God is the best organizing idea or unifying concept to make sense of the world.

I hope I have answered your questions. Let me know your response. Don't you, with your scientific bent, seek a unifying concept to explain the universe?

Love to Sylvia.

> Your friend,
>
> Bill

 C3 C3 80 80

May 6, 1991

Dear Mort,

You have not answered the question I put to you in a recent letter, "Why is there something rather than nothing? Why?"

Yesterday, I attended a lecture by a leading Jewish theologian. He made an interesting point. Take someone like yourself, for example. Why do you spend time visiting a prison and helping the prisoners? On what basis do you have these values? What are you reaching for? Why not spend your retirement just relaxing? Does not your quest for values and doing good deeds presuppose a higher ground of value (i.e., something Divine) to which you are responding, even though you deny its existence?

By the way, on whom is the burden of proof (in a logical, not a scientific, sense)—the atheist or the theist?

I look forward to hearing from you.

Love to Sylvia.

Your friend,

Bill

CS CS SO SO

May 7, 1991

Dear Bill,

I note from your letter of May 3 that you are back from your Rabbinical Convention. I hope that you had an enjoyable time. What do rabbis talk about at these meetings? Are rabbis of all persuasions there, and if so are there discussions about the merits of the various denominations?

To your letter: "Larger meaning." What a lovely expression! The assumption of (or perhaps the desire for) a larger meaning seems to be the engine driving belief. Without this larger meaning, life, the world, eternity—these all become rather bleak for the believer. He will say,

"You mean that we are born, we live, and we die, and *that* is all?" The believer has to believe that *that* is not all, that there is a larger meaning (a Higher Power?) and that, therefore, life, the world, eternity *are* meaningful (whatever that means). And because his own existence is meaningless *to him*, he has to believe that at least something is meaningful, and so he believes.

When two scientists at the University of Utah recently announced that they had accomplished cold fusion, laboratories throughout the world attempted to duplicate their results in their own labs independently, i.e., without in any way working with the original researchers. As it turned out, the results were not independently verifiable.

In your fourth paragraph, you come dangerously close to my position that God, a Higher Power, religion, a larger meaning, etc., are all myths. May I quote my friend *Webster's* again? "myth: a person or thing having only an imaginary or unverifiable existence; an ill-founded belief held uncritically, especially by an interested group." You say that religion is more like an art than science. It bears not the slightest resemblance to either. It is pure myth.

You ask how does one independently verify that Beethoven or Michelangelo was a genius. First, it depends upon one's definition of the word *genius*. This is quite arbitrary. If they fit this definition, then they are geniuses. It is as simple as that. We do not have to verify (independently or otherwise) whether they are geniuses. We have set certain standards for creativity and for genius, and when these standards are met, that is that. This is really not *ad rem*. Whether or not Beethoven and Michelangelo come up to the standards of creative genius is really a matter of opinion—even though probably 99 percent of educated opinion would agree. It is still, however, a matter of opinion. Would you accept the existence of God as a matter of opinion? You claim it is a matter of fact.

Coming back to Rabbi Kaplan's "will to live": I have the will to live the "maximum life." Does that make me a believer?

You say that Maimonides held that we can only know God's negative attributes. What are God's negative attributes?

My nomination for the Gobbledegook Prize of the Week goes to the statement, "Other thinkers, such as Whitehead and Hartshorne, claim that, through reason, we can transcend ourselves and know God as the pattern of all possibility and the synthesis of all actuality."

Their belief (as you state it) is that the idea of God is the best organizing idea or unifying concept to make sense of the world. And here I thought that was the job of science. As a matter of fact, shortly before his death, Albert Einstein was working on a "unifying concept" of the universe, one general overall theory which would hold within itself all of the laws of the universe. Of course, that had nothing whatever to do with God, process theology, larger meaning, or any theology or mythology.

All the best.

Your friend,

Mort

14

Wouldn't It Be Odd if Religion Was a Complete and Total Self-Deception?

April 30, 1991

Dear Mort,

On the way to our Rabbinical Convention here at the Concord, I stopped to eat lunch at Friendly's in Middletown, Connecticut. Sitting at the counter, I started a conversation with the gentleman sitting next to me, who turned out to be an electrical engineer who was also a fundamentalist. I asked him how he reconciled the two. He replied: "No problem. Science deals with the material world, religion with the spiritual dimension."

Here at the convention, one of the sessions dealt with Maimonides. Maimonides maintained what he called "negative theology." God is totally unlike man. We can only know what God is not, not what God is.

Sitting in the lobby of the Concord, watching my fellow rabbis pass by, skullcaps on their heads, I ask: Wouldn't

it be odd if religion was a complete and total self-deception, with nothing at all to it? The common consent of
mankind is something to be reckoned with, don't you
think?

All the best.

Bill

CB CB BO BO

May 2, 1991

Dear Bill,

Your letter of April 30 tells about the fundamentalist Christian engineer who you met and questioned about how
he reconciled science and religion. You state that he said
that God created nature and science explains that nature.
If you examine these two points carefully you will note
that they reconcile nothing. Your engineer simply said
that a supernatural Being created the universe. He made
no statement explaining in scientific (logical, rational)
terms as to how this fits in with his scientific approach to
the universe. This is a perfect example of the compart-
mentalizing that I object to so strongly. Why would a
rational man apply logic and reasoning to everything in
the world with the exception of God and religion? Why
does his mind have two compartments: one for God,
which is immune to objective thought and analysis, and
the other for everything else that he observes analytically
and rationally?

You state that Maimonides' "negative theology" claims
that we can only know what God is not and never know
what God is. All of the theologians whom you have cited

so far seem to dispute this. They all seem to have a copy of God's personal résumé.

In your letter you muse (on seeing all of the rabbis with their *kipot*[1]) about how odd it would be "if religion were a total self-delusion and self-deception." It would not be at all odd. History is rife with examples of massive self-deception and self-delusion, from the Crusades, Shabbetai Tzvi, the German people under Hitler, up to too many examples in our times to cite. Mass self-deception is *not* unusual.

All the best to the Kaufmans.

Your friend,

Mort

---

1. Head coverings also known as *yarmulkes*.

15

How Do We Know Our Cognitive Powers Are Reliable Unless We Believe in God as the Ultimate Knower of Truth?

May 14, 1991

Dear Mort,

I attended a lecture yesterday delivered by a well-known theistic philosopher named Alvin Plantinga.

He advanced an evolutionary argument against naturalism based on Darwin's doubt. Darwin stated: "With me, the horrid doubt always arises whether the convictions of man's mind, which has been developed from the mind of the lower animals, are of any value or at all trustworthy. Would anyone trust in the convictions of a monkey's mind, if there are any convictions in such a mind?"

The question raised is: How do you know that your cognitive faculties are reliable *unless* you posit the existence of a Supreme Being who is trustworthy and who guarantees the truth of our clear and distinct ideas, because

113

He created us in His image (i.e., with the capacity to reason).

If you reject this argument (which I am sure you will), how do you know your cognitive faculties are reliable in denying the existence of the Deity?

All the best.

Your friend,

Bill

C? C? ?? ??

May 16, 1991

Dear Bill,

I like the questions (propositions?) which you (pro)pose in your letter of May 14 because I find it so easy to poke holes in them. You ask, "How do you know that your cognitive faculties are reliable *unless* you posit the existence of a Supreme Being who is trustworthy and who guarantees the truth of our clear and distinct ideas, because He created us in His image (i.e., with the capacity to reason)."

My reply takes the form of a few simple "counter questions" and a few not quite so simple.

The Simple Questions

1. How do you *know* that there is a Supreme Being?

2. Assuming a Supreme Being, how do you *know* that He created us in His image?

3. Assuming that He created us in His image, how do you *know* that this image includes the capacity to reason? (*Dayenu!*)

The Others

1. Why do you assume that a Supreme Being who has permitted such horrendous events to befall man (the Spanish Inquisition, the Crusades, the Holocaust, the Soviet Gulag, the Bangladesh Typhoon of 1991, *ad infinitum*) is trustworthy?

2. What is the connection between the reliability of my cognitive faculties and a "trustworthy" Supreme Being?

3. Why do you deem it necessary to prove the reliability of your mind in connection with a Supreme Being?

And finally to your last question, which is really the clincher:

4. How do you know your cognitive faculties are reliable in denying the existence of the Deity?

As I have stated repeatedly, I cannot prove the nonexistence of God nor can I prove the nonexistence of a dog with seven legs. I cannot (and do not) deny the existence of either. I simply state that, lacking IVE of any kind, I will assume that neither of these exists until such time as IVE of the existence of either of them is presented.

You can only assume one of two alternatives: either my cognitive faculties are reliable or they are not. If you assume that they are reliable, then your question has no validity and is out of order. If, on the other hand, you assume that they are not reliable, then we have no discussion and we have been wasting paper, postage, and time. If you, in effect, say that I am mentally unqualified to think about this question (and I am sure that there are some who would say that), then, of course, that ends our whole dialogue.

Okay, Bill, the ball is in your court.

Still your friend,

Mort

CZ CZ ED ED

May 23, 1991

Dear Mort,

In my letter of May 14, I was proposing a philosophical, not a personal, issue. I have the utmost respect for your cognitive faculties. In fact, you are one of the brightest people I know.

I'm sure that you would consider Einstein rather intelligent too! Well, Einstein once said that the mystery of the universe lies in the comprehensibility. That is the point I was trying to make. Einstein was saying, I think, that the fact that our cognitive faculties *are* capable of understanding much about the universe indicates a higher, Divine intelligence because of the harmony between our minds and the world. Einstein, you may recall, said that he believed in Spinoza's God, who is revealed in the *harmony* of the universe, and not in a God who rewards and punishes. Does it carry any weight with you that Einstein, who knew much more about the universe than virtually anyone, believed in a Supreme Being or intelligence?

In response to your specific questions:

1. I do not *know* that there is a Supreme Being; I believe that it is more reasonable to posit or affirm a Higher Intelligence than to deny it. Why? Because the universe cries out for an explanation, and chance is no explanation.

2. I, too, am bothered by the problem of evil—the Holocaust, the Gulag, etc. These have resulted from man's misuse of his free will. I do not know why God permits such horrors, but clearly if God made a primordial decision to give us free will, He is not going to reverse it and intervene at all times.

As I indicated in my previous letter, the God hypothesis differs from the seven-legged dog in these respects:

1. God is alleged to be real, people have claimed to have experienced God, and the concept of God is not self-contradictory.

2. In contrast, no one alleges that a seven-legged dog is real; it is totally imaginary. No one claims to have experienced it. A dog by definition has four legs; a seven-legged dog is a self-contradictory concept.

How do you respond to this? Moreover, you do not have IVE for the external world or the existence of other minds.

In answer to your biblical question, the dialogue between God and Moses wherein Moses asks God His name is in chapter 3 of the Book of Exodus, verses 13, 14ff.

Incidentally, if you are so sure there is no God, why are you so bothered by the problem of evil? The problem of evil only arises if one posits a God who is both omnipotent and perfectly good. If God is in the same category as a seven-legged dog, there is no problem of evil.

Warmest wishes to Sylvia.

Your friend,

Bill

16

Unproven Assumptions and the Analogy of the Seven-Legged Dog

May 10, 1991

Dear Mort,

In your recent letter, you assume that logic, reasoning, and proof must be applied to all things. However, even the most rational, logical, and analytical philosophers must accept at least one unproven assumption or axiom.

Consider, for example, the contemporary atheist philosopher Sidney Hook. His point of view is very much like yours; he thinks that "God" belongs in the category of elves, fairies, gremlins, seven-legged dogs, etc. In an essay entitled "Naturalism and First Principles," Hook admits: "Since every philosophic position must start somewhere and make some preliminary or initial assumptions that can be challenged at least verbally by other philosophers, it is always possible to level the charge of circularity."[1]

---

1. Sidney Hook, "Naturalism and First Principles," in *The Quest for Being* (Buffalo, NY: Prometheus Books, 1991), p. 176.

Your point of view is based on the following unproven assumptions:

 1. Science is the only reliable form of knowledge. (Hook makes this assumption too.)

 2. Therefore, you *a priori* limit reality to that which is observed, observable, or the effect of some entity (like black holes, etc.) alleged to exist by scientists.

 3. The burden of proof is on the theist.

The theist makes these assumptions:

 1. Other forms of knowledge are possible: personal knowledge (I know you, etc.), mystical knowledge, revelation, etc. (I say *possible*, not always reliable. You don't even admit the *possibility* of other forms of knowledge.)

 2. Reality is far richer than science can describe.

 3. The burden of proof is on the atheist because there is an initial presumption in favor of God, since "God" has a regular use in our language and is part of an ancient and venerated form of life. Moreover, it appears that there is at least as much order as chance in the universe. The burden of proof is on the atheist who goes against the axiom of intelligibility in arguing that the *whole universe* is a product of chance.

Let me know if I have correctly identified your *unproven* assumptions or presuppositions.

In my opinion, the basis of our debate is that we hold different unproven and unprovable assumptions. I main-

tain that my assumptions have more beneficial consequences for the conduct of life; you maintain yours do.
I hold that my position is more reasonable because I am
open to *all* possibilities. You are *not* open to the possibility of the existence of a Deity. You are more *dogmatic*
than I am.

I think we have reached the essence of our debate.

Looking forward to hearing from you.

Your friend,

Bill

Ω Ω Ω Ω

May 13, 1991

Dear Bill,

In your letter of May 10 you state, "However, even the
most rational, logical, and analytical philosophers must
accept at least one unproven assumption or axiom."

I cannot speak about philosophers, but I do know that the
axioms and "unproven assumptions" that scientists assume all have one common feature. The logic that employs
the axiom as a starting point *always* arrives at a scientific and demonstrable truth, fact, or reality. And what is
the nature of that reality? It is independently verifiable. The
philosopher (theologian) may assume that God is the
source of redemption, that God is a process, that God is
this, that, and the other thing, but his unproven assumptions float in the air unconnected to any reality.

Responding to your claim that my point of view is based upon three unproven assumptions:

1. Science *is* the only reliable form of knowledge. Let us ask my old friend *Webster's* again: Science—possession of knowledge as distinguished from ignorance and misunderstanding; knowledge covering general truths on the operation of general laws, *especially as obtained and tested by scientific method* (my emphasis). No, Bill, I simply say that science is the only reliable form of knowledge of the physical universe and its components.

2. Therefore, you say, I limit reality to what is observed and observable. Again, I refer to only the physical world.

3. Your last claim of my unproven assumptions is that the burden of proof is on the atheist. This is so obviously untrue that I cannot see you using it as an argument. The one who claims the existence of the seven-legged dog has the burden of proof.

To elaborate on the above: I have never denied that there are forms of knowledge beyond the scientific. Here, I use the word *knowledge* in its broadest sense. This might be called "emotional knowledge," i.e., not emotional in the pejorative sense but in the sense of dealing with emotions. Love, honor, fear, loyalty, hatred, cynicism, etc., all can be thought of as parts of knowledge, stretching the term a bit, but it is knowledge of another kind. I do not deny this kind of knowledge but I do deny vehemently what you call mystical knowledge and revelation.

You say that "reality is far richer than science can describe." I am not sure that I know what you mean by this, but as a student of science I can assure you that the scientific descriptions of reality are far more beautiful and richer than the fantasies that religion makes of reality. If you mean that the literature of religions is richer than that of science, I have two responses: (1) You are really not into the literature of science, and (2) Hans Christian Andersen, the Brothers Grimm, and even Stephen King are richer in their literature.

Do you seriously mean that we should accept the concept of God because it has been around for so many millennia? How about the flat earth? How about the universe being made up of four elements? How about the earth being the center of the universe?

You say, "There is at least as much order as chance in the universe." First, neither you nor I know this to be true, and second, there is really no contradiction between order and chance. It is purely by chance that the universe is ordered.

I am sorry Bill, but you have not identified my unproven assumptions. I do not assume that there is a dog with seven legs. That is not the same as saying that I assume that there is no seven-legged dog. I simply await IVE that that dog exists. I do not assume that there is no God. I simply await IVE that there is a God. If there is a God, prove it!

I do not claim that my waiting to be shown proof (*not* my unprovable assumption) has more or less beneficial consequences for the conduct of life. I ask, rather, "If a lie has more beneficial consequences for life, should one tell the truth?"

You really are not open to all possibilities as you say you are. You do not accept the possibility that there is no God.

I, on the other hand, do not claim that there is no God. I simply say that as of now no one has been able to prove that there is a God, and until that can be proved I will have to assume (as I do with my pet dog) that there is none.

Now what?

Your friend,

Mort

May 17, 1991

Dear Mort,

I still claim that you are operating with concealed assumptions.

1. The claim that science is the only reliable form of knowledge conceals the metaphysical assumptions that everything which is said to exist must be perceptible or capable of being scientifically described or characterized. This is an assumption. Is there not humanistic knowledge? Aren't there other forms of discourse than science?

2. You yourself say that you refer only to the physical world. Is the physical world all there is? Are there not spiritual realities? Is it not an *unproven* assumption to claim that they do not exist?

3. You state and therefore assume: "It is purely by chance that the universe is ordered." You assume

that chance is the basis of order. I assume that God is. How can you say that yours is less of an assumption than mine?

4. On the burden of proof issue: It is more irrational to say that the universe is just there (by chance, if you will) than to say that the universe cries out for an explanation. When did you ever *perceive* something emerging from absolute nothingness?

5. As far as proof is concerned, here is a proof for the existence of God:
    a. If life has meaning, there is a God.
    b. Life has meaning.
    c. Therefore, there is a God. (You can see from this that proof is not worth much.)

This is a *valid* proof, but the atheist will not accept it because he denies the premise that life has meaning.

As far as the principles of IVE that you stress so much: Can you independently verify that there is an external world? That there are other minds?

Your hallowed principles of proof and IVE are useful for technology but do not take us very far philosophically.

Love to Sylvia. Happy Shavuos.

Your friend,

Bill

ෆ ෆ ౸ ౸

May 21, 1991

Dear Bill,

Of course, as you say in yours of May 17, I make assumptions. These are assumptions, however, upon which I can base a chain of logic and arrive at an IVE fact. (From *Webster's*: fact—something that has actual existence.)

Replying to the numbered points in your letter:

1. I am sure that you will agree that science is the only reliable form of knowledge about *facts*. I do not know the meaning of the term *humanistic knowledge*, but I assume that you mean knowledge of feelings and emotions. Of course, these exist and their manifestations are measurable by EKGs, blood pressure devices, polygraphs, etc. Their *manifestations* are measurable. The "humanistic knowledge" itself is not. What in the world has that got to do with the existence of a Higher Power?

2. I have never denied the existence of spiritual realities. I consider myself a man of deep spiritual sensibilities. I love music, the arts, etc. I am deeply moved by the beauties of nature. I am an emotional person. I love and I hate. But what has all of that to do with elves, hobgoblins, and a Higher Power?

3. I assume that the universe is the result of chance, and you assume that it is the result of God. Why do I consider my assumption more valid than yours? First, I assume that the universe was created by "nothing." You find it necessary to postulate an inventor

with an infinitely complex mind and, to believe the modern theologians, with an ethic and a conscience. My "nothing" is so much simpler that it can hardly be called an assumption.

4. Referring to the "burden of proof" question, neither you nor I have proof of our theories. I simply say that I do not know while you claim God, again with no IVE.

Of course, we have never witnessed something emerging from nothing. There are probably innumerable things that we have never witnessed including infinity. And we have never witnessed the creation—if there ever was such a thing.

5. My objection to your "valid proof" is that you state, "If life has meaning, there is a God." This is a *non sequitur* and, in my case, demonstrably false. My life has meaning, but meaning which *I* give it. What can be the value of the meaning if one must look outside oneself for it?

Can I verify independently that there are other minds and that there is an external world? If and when our correspondence is read by others, that will constitute independent verification that we have minds. What do you mean by an external world?

Your final paragraph belittles philosophy. You state that IVE is useful for technology but does not take us very far philosophically. If your philosophical concept cannot stand up to rigid, logical examination, of what value is it? Are you indulging in the compartmentalization of the mind that I rail against? Do you apply strict rules of logic to everything except philosophical concepts and think of philosophy in terms of faith, belief, and nonrational ideation?

Love to Nathalie. Happy May 21!

Your friend,

Mort

Read the Charts:

YOUR CHART			MY CHART	
God	Seven-Legged Dog		God	Seven-Legged Dog
Alleged to be real	Imaginary		Alleged to exist	Alleged to exist by those who see pink elephants
People claim to have experienced	No claim of experience		People claim to have experienced	See above
Not self-contradictory	Self-contradictory since a dog is a four-legged canine		Replete with contradictions	No more contradictory than a man with twelve toes; it depends on definition

May 25, 1991

Dear Bill,

This may sound like the old routine of "After you, Alfonse!" "No, after *you*, Gaston!"—but I did not for one moment think that you were questioning my cognitive faculties in your recent letter.

What is the connection between (a) the fact that our cognitive faculties *are* capable of understanding much about the universe and (b) the existence of a higher, Divine intelligence? And what is the meaning of the phrase, "the harmony between our minds and the world"?

Einstein, along with some of the most brilliant thinkers in the world, believed (and believe) in some kind of Supreme Being. We can never know what parental influences or what childhood experiences led them to the practice of compartmentalization of the mind. I know little about contemporary philosophers, but I imagine that God can get testimonials from many (if not most) of them. This simply indicates that the vast majority of people are believers—for whatever cause. (Note that I do not say "for whatever reason.")

As sincerely as you believe (not *know*) that chance is not an explanation of the universe, I believe (also not know) that it is the best explanation. You say that God made a primordial decision to give man free will and that evil is man's misuse of that free will. Now you really have me confused about your God. You have been referring to God as "the power that makes for salvation" and as a process and in a variety of other ways. Are you now going back to the anthropomorphic God who "made" man (in his image) and gave him free will? And if God did give man free will, do you not think that when one considers the results of man's misuse of free will that God may have made a very serious error?

God is alleged to be real by people who have compartmentalized their minds, people who have, in effect, been brainwashed. People who have been brainwashed by excessive alcohol have seen pink elephants, if not seven-legged dogs.

I do not accept the statements of people who claim to have had religious experiences involving God, and I do not think you do either. Rabbi Mordecai Kaplan rejects this kind of experience as arrant nonsense.

If you think that God is not self-contradictory, refer to *Finding God* by Sonsino and Syme and tell me which of the ten different Gods is the real One.

I have never alleged that a seven-legged dog is real. What I have said is that one cannot prove that it does not exist. Some years ago the Soviets grafted (for want of a better word) a second head onto a dog. I saw films of the dog on television. Both heads seemed to behave normally. If I substituted the two-headed dog for my seven-legged one, would your logic still hold?

I am bothered by evil, not by the problem of evil. The problem of evil is a problem only for the believer. I love the problem of evil because it makes God so much more difficult to explain, to justify, to posit, etc.

Now what?

All the best.

Your friend,

Mort

Cஃ Cஃ கூ கூ

May 30, 1991

Dear Mort,

I don't think that I made my point clear about proof.

What I was trying to show is that proof isn't always enough. The example I gave is:

1. If life has meaning, there is a God.

2. Life has meaning.

3. Therefore, there is a God.

If you accept premises 1 and 2, this *is* a valid proof (valid means: if the premises are true, the conclusion must be true also).

What is problematic here are the premises.

The underlying point I am trying to get at is that the important thing is not proof but rather understanding what our underlying premises are.

Your underlying premise is that matter and energy are ultimate.

Mine is that God is ultimate. Neither of these premises can be proved. They are assumptions, ultimate presuppositions.

In response to your letter of May 25, please make clear to me how chance can be the very best explanation for the universe. Also, the fact that different people have various ideas of God does not prove that the idea of God is self-contradictory.

All the best.

Your friend,

Bill

ଔ ଔ ଚ ଚ

June 1, 1991

Dear Bill,

I don't like getting caught up in semantics about the term *valid proof*, but the term is ambiguous. On the one hand, *Webster's* says, "valid—having a conclusion directly derived from premises," which was the sense in which you used the term. On the other hand, *Webster's* says, "valid—well grounded, sound." And it is in this sense that I said your proof is invalid.

Yes, my underlying premise is that matter and energy are ultimate (basic, fundamental). I accept this premise because all of the observable phenomena in the universe (except the creation) are explainable based on this premise.

Your premise is that God is ultimate, but *none* of the events of the universe is explainable based upon this premise unless one believes in miracles. Regarding the creation, I refer you to one of your recent letters wherein you state that something cannot arise from nothing. God, therefore, could not have created the universe from nothing, and as a matter of fact, how could God Himself have come about from nothingness?

I believe (repeat, not *know*) that chance is the best explanation for the universe because it is the most logical and scientific explanation of the universe as we know it.

If the universe comprises everything, is your God a part of the universe? And if God created the universe, can we assume, then, that He created Himself? No, Bill, this is not self-contradictory, it is impossible.

The various concepts of God remind me of the fable of the three blind men who encounter an elephant and who then proceed to describe it as a rope, a tree, and a wall. If there is a God, just what is He? Which God are you talking about? In the words of that quiz show host, "Will the real God please stand up."

Finally, Bill, I must repeat my old complaint. I raise questions in my letters which you do not (cannot) answer. Please go back over mine of May 16, 21, and 26 and let me have your answers.

Love to Nathalie and the crew!

Your friend,

Mort

17

Summary, Response, and Critique

June 3, 1991

Dear Mort,

Here is a summary of some of the main points I have been trying to make.

First, I have underscored the point that the question of the existence and nature of God is not a scientific question but rather a metascientific or metaphysical issue. It is not like looking for a quasar or a black hole—or a seven-legged dog. (The scientist Freeman Dyson in *Infinite in All Directions* also says that it is a metascientific question.) As such, it is a matter of one's ultimate or basic presuppositions.

Now if, as I think you do, one restricts one's discourse only to the scientific (where IVE is possible), then one is working with the presupposition or assumption of the omnicompetence of science. You refuse to admit that this is an assumption. Rather, you operate as if science and only science is the whole truth. What I am trying to do, in part, is to get you to admit that this is an assumption.

You asked me in a previous letter the difference between logical and scientific proof. "Logical" includes both inductive and deductive reasoning; science consists only of inductive reasoning.

Example of deductive reasoning:
  All men are mortal. Socrates is a man. Therefore, Socrates is mortal.
Example of inductive reasoning:
  Every swan I have ever seen is white. Therefore, all swans are white.

Now, science is based on inductive reasoning and probability. Science cannot give you absolute certainty that you will not see a black swan tomorrow. So, also, science cannot give you certainty that there is no God.

What then is the crux of the issue?

The crux of the issue is the axiom of intelligibility (the assumption that the universe makes sense).

I hold that the existence of God is a better explanation for the universe than chance, because God as a unifying concept, referring to a supreme unitary actuality, renders the world intelligible in the following ways:

1. It renders the universe a unity, a whole.

2. It offers a unified explanation for the unified order of the world in terms of a cosmic mind.

3. It explains the feeling many people have of being ultimately dependent for their existence upon a Higher Power.

4. It explains the feeling many people have, that the entire universe depends for its existence upon a Being which has aseity, self-existence, or necessary existence, i.e., independent existence, existence from itself.

5. It explains why so many people have claimed to have had religious experiences, mystical experiences, etc. It explains the religious testimony given in the Bible.

6. It explains why ethical imperatives seem to have an ultimacy not reducible to human feelings.

Now, as I see it, you reject the axiom of intelligibility. You have argued that the universe is a product of chance and need not be intelligible.

I argue that if the world is not intelligible, our human minds are an incredible freak of nature and our human existence is totally absurd and gratuitous.

Therefore, I hold as a working assumption (always subject to revision, which I don't think your assumption of the omnicompetence of science is) that there is a God, i.e., a Universal Mind that renders the universe intelligible.

Looking forward to your rebuttals.

Your friend,

Bill

June 6, 1991

Dear Bill,

I must admit that, in a real sense, I am making an assumption when I say that everything in the universe is or will be explainable by science (logic, reason, intellect). It is an assumption in the same sense that $2 + 2 = 4$ is an assumption. And, of course, my assumption can be proven by IVE.

Why, then, can I not accept your assumption that "There are more things in heaven and earth, Horatio, than are dreamed of by our philosophers"? Because if I accept your assumption as valid, I cannot reject the assumption of elves and hobgoblins, of Santa Claus and the Tooth Fairy. And, somewhat more rational, of the religious fundamentalists (Jewish, Islamic, and Christian). And there is no reason (rationale) for believing any of these (including your) assumptions. And because, based upon these false assumptions, sound logic brings us to a false conclusion.

Shortly before his death, Albert Einstein was working on a unified (and unifying) theory of the universe. He believed that he could come up with one law, one unitary law, which would be the basis and explanation of every physical phenomenon in the universe. Einstein's view of the universe (which I, of course, accept) is not one of chaos but one of order—but statistical order (one could say, "of chance order"). But these laws do not conflict with each other. They work together and make sense. Einstein's goal was to find the one law, "the unifying concept" (to borrow your words), that ties together all of the laws of the universe.

You hold that God is a better explanation of the universe because it is so easy to explain everything if one assumes God. You cannot accept the situation where you cannot find the simple explanation, so you invent God.

Let us see how your six reasons for assuming that God renders the world intelligible stack up to logic.

1. You say that the existence of God "renders the universe a unity, a whole." Modern science conceives of the universe in this way without the necessity of injecting God into the picture.

2. You attribute the "unified order of the world" to a cosmic mind. This is a repetition of your first point. Why invent a "cosmic mind" when science explains the universe without it?

3. Is the world rendered more intelligible because, as you state, the existence of God "explains the feeling many people have of being ultimately dependent for their existence upon a Higher Power"? Or is this feeling that people have merely the result of childhood brainwashing or superstition?

4. To paraphrase Rabbi Kaufman: Do you know of anything ever arising from nothing? Whence God?

5. Do you still believe in miracles?

6. I absolutely reject your statement that "ethical imperatives seem to have an ultimacy not reducible to human feelings." God could not have given man his sense of good and evil. As Bertrand Russell put it:

"For those who believe that God is the source of morality, that He has told man what is good and what is evil, one must ask: If God has separated good from evil, then, to Him, there is no difference. He has had to say what is good and what is evil. If on the other hand, you say that God is good, then good and evil are independent of God's decision."

I am fairly certain that you will agree with me that there is just as much immorality among the religious as among the atheists. If God's purpose is to show man the right path, either He or religion has, obviously, failed—after working at it for about five thousand years.

I do not reject the axiom of intelligibility. I aver that the universe is a product of chance and *is* intelligible. (From *Webster's*: intelligible—1. capable of being understood or comprehended; 2. apprehensible by the *intellect only* [my emphasis].)

Unless you reject Darwin, you must agree that *all* evolutionary progress is dependent upon what you call freaks of nature, and this includes man.

Really, Bill, it seems to me that all of your six points boil down to one, the old point that since you cannot conceive of how or why the universe came about, you invent God as a nice easy answer.

Now what?

Love to the family.

Your friend,

Mort

June 3, 1991

Dear Mort,

Thanks for sending me the letter to the editor of the *New York Times* about the present status of rabbis. I agree with it. The article the letter criticizes was too good to be true.

Here is my reply to your letter of June 1.

My point with respect to a valid argument is that you can have a valid argument which is not sound, so proof doesn't always amount to much. For a conclusion to be *true*, the argument must be valid and sound (i.e., the premises must be true), which was not the case in the argument I presented.

The only miracle I believe in is the universe itself. No one has yet given a scientific explanation of where the first molecule or the Big Bang or the universe itself came from. (Whichever theory you accept—Big Bang or Eternal Universe—even if the universe is eternal, *it could* still depend on God for its existence.)

Until science does this, I will continue to believe in creation or God's eternal creativity. My God is not part of the universe; He/She comprises the universe and is more than the universe. This view is known as panentheism, which means that the universe is *in* God (as opposed to pantheism, in which the universe equals God). As we are to the amoeba, so God is to us.

It is neither impossible nor self-contradictory to assert that God created Himself/Herself. The process philosopher Charles Hartshorne asserts just this. I don't agree with him, but it's not impossible. Creation for me is simply a miracle.

Will the real God please stand up! This is the question I have been wrestling with all my life and am still wrestling with. Let us remember that "God" is a word, symbol, or metaphor that represents ultimate reality. By ultimate reality I mean the eternal, final reality that existed before or with all universes and will exist after all universes perish (if they do) or with them if they do not.

For you, ultimate reality is nothingness. For me, ultimate reality is God. (If you are right, God is nothingness and we have no ultimate hope. I *hope* you are wrong.)

For me, God is ultimate reality, the Supreme Being, which I hold is Mind.

The entry in the *Encyclopaedia Judaica* on "God" says that more important than God's power, in Judaism, is His *wisdom*.

For me, God is the ultimate wisdom. I know not (what it's all about) but He/She knows the ultimate meaning.

There is a medieval Jewish statement: "If I knew God, I would be Him." How could I possibly know the real God? My belief is that a real God exists, but our concepts are metaphors, symbols, approximations.

There is a mystical saying: "A God we would fully comprehend would not be a God." That is, a God we could prove by IVE would not be a God.

Note, thus, the uniqueness of religious language; i.e., if we could prove the existence of God, or know it with certainty, the whole religion language game would collapse, for *faith* would then lose its meaning.

Looking forward to hearing from you.

Your friend,

Bill

C03 C03 80 80

June 18, 1991

Dear Mort,

As I have said repeatedly, I do not claim to *know* anything about God.

Formulating an idea of God is an attempt to say what reality must be like if the demand for the rational intelligibility of the world is to be satisfied. That is, the idea of God represents what a total and complete explanation of the universe (or universes) would be like.

Your position is that there is no ultimate reality and therefore no ultimate intelligibility. I would like to think that there is.

The problem of the Divine attributes is a very difficult one, and I do not claim to have solved it. But I do not predicate attributes arbitrarily. What I do is extrapolate from the best qualities we know to determine what a Supreme Mind or Supreme Being would be like (this is the method of analogy).

The other approach is that of Maimonides, who said that we cannot predicate any positive attributes of God, only negative attributes (saying what God is not) and attributes of action (i.e., specifying what are to count as manifestations of God).

Do you like Maimonides better? The other problem you ask about is anthropomorphism. "He" and "She" I regard as anthropomorphisms. I do not believe God has a gender.

I used to believe that we could only predicate concepts like "force" or "process" to God. However, I now realize that all human thought is anthropomorphic. Hence, terms like *force* or *process* are anthropomorphic too. So, I now believe that we ought to predicate of God the qualities that represent the best we know: wisdom, all-inclusiveness, mind, knowledge of the ultimate meaning, etc.

I do not believe that God created Itself. This is someone else's view. I cited it to show that it *is* possible to believe that. My view is that God is eternal—always existent.

I believe that one God is more logical than many gods, because the Unity of God accounts better for the harmony of the universe.

Again, I do not know these things as facts. My idea of God is simply a religious hypothesis that would constitute the best explanation for the universe if the universe *is* ultimately intelligible.

The *act of faith* is to believe that it is ultimately intelligible.

Incidentally, the universe could be *infinite in all directions* (this is the title of the physicist Freeman Dyson's book, who *also* believes in a God inherent in the universe, growing in wisdom and knowledge) and still require a Divinity to sustain it. The attempted proofs of the existence of God of Maimonides and Aquinas do not presuppose creation. Even if the universe is eternal, it could still be dependent upon God for its existence.

I want to make clear what the method of analogy is. Take, for example, God's wisdom. God's wisdom, in one respect, is greater than any wisdom we can conceive. But it must have some analogy or some likeness to human wisdom, or it would make no sense to refer to it at all. So, by analogous predication we attribute wisdom to God. (So you see that it is not simply a crude anthropomorphism, but a refined one, if you will.)

All of these topics—analogy, Divine attributes, anthropomorphism, the ultimate intelligibility of the universe—are controversial subjects in the philosophy of religion.

The only point I am making is that your position is as controversial as mine. Your assumption that there is no God is as much of a presupposition as my belief that there is. Both are interpretations. Do you accept that?

If you do, then we determine what the best explanation or interpretation is in terms of criteria such as consistency, coherence with experience, pragmatic value, etc.

Looking forward to hearing from you.

All the best to Sylvia.

> Your friend,
>
> Bill

CB CB &D &D

Dear Bill,

In the past I have repeatedly complained about the practice of the theologians of listing God's attributes as though
they had read His résumé. They never give us any factual
basis for their descriptions of who God is and what He is
like. And here I am *not* talking about their supplying IVE,
but only some reason for saying that God is this or God
is that.

I am listing below the statements which you make in your
recent letter that suffer from the same absence of basis.

1. "My God is not part of the universe. He/She comprises the universe and is more than the universe."

2. "The universe is *in* God."

3. "It is neither impossible nor self-contradictory to
assert that God created Himself/Herself." (Explain
how it is possible since you stated that something
cannot come from nothing. First cause?!)

4. "God is the ultimate wisdom." (Anthropomorphism?)

5. "He/She knows the ultimate meaning." (But
in the same letter you say that He *is* the ultimate

meaning. Which one? Also, how can He know anything?)

Can you tell me how you know all of these "facts" about
God? Can you tell me if you have any more substantial
reason to believe all of this than the Greeks had to believe in the characters and characteristics of their gods?
As a matter of fact, if we are seeking a more logical, more
rational theology, the division of labor which the Greeks
gave to their pantheon makes a good deal more sense. If
you are going to believe in the supernatural, be practical; give every god his due.

As far as ultimate realities are concerned, you misread my
position. My ultimate reality is not nothingness.

Accepting your definition that the ultimate reality is what
existed before the universe existed and what will exist
after the universe ceases to exist, I claim that there is no
such thing as an ultimate reality, since the universe always existed and always will exist. As I like to put it, "Infinity in both directions."

Finally, quoting so-called experts proves nothing. There
are so-called experts on both sides of the case. I am re-
minded of the court trial, where each side produces expert witnesses to bolster his case. Nothing is proven by
this technique.

Where do we go from here?

All the best to the family.

Your friend,

Mort

June 13, 1991

Dear Mort,

Here are my replies to your criticisms of my thesis that the idea of God renders the world intelligible.

1. You write: "Modern science conceives of the universe (as a whole, a unity) without the necessity of injecting God into the picture." You adduce as evidence Albert Einstein, whose goal was to find the one law, the unifying concept, that ties together all laws in the universe.

My reply: This same Einstein said: "I believe in Spinoza's God, who reveals Himself in the harmony of all being, not in a God who concerns Himself with the fate and actions of men." Einstein evidently saw the necessity of injecting God into the picture. I agree with Einstein on this point.

2. I am not "inventing" a cosmic mind. The stopping point of explanation for you is a law of nature. For the theist, the natural stopping place for explanation is a cosmic mind or agent.

A law of nature describes how things operate. Only a cosmic mind or agent can explain *existence*. Science explains the operation of but not the existence of the universe. I simply hold that a cosmic mind is the best ultimate explanation. This is a metaphysical hypothesis; whether it is invented or real is precisely the point at issue.

3. The feeling of dependence on a Higher Power is both learned and innate. Otherwise religion would not be universal.

4. God does not arise from nothing. The theist holds that God is eternal; He *always* existed.

5. As I said, the one miracle I believe in is the creation or *existence* of the universe. (If it's eternal.)

6. The question of whether ethics requires religious justification is an old and controversial issue.

If you accept evolution as you do, how did man, a freak of nature, learn ethics? I think it makes sense to attribute the ultimate origin of whatever ethical sense man has (and it's not very impressive) to a Higher Power.

With respect to intelligibility, *Webster's* defines *chance* as "without *apparent* cause or design," that is, unexplained, *unintelligible*! To find the cause or design would be to render it intelligible.

With reference to your questions of May 16, 21, and 26: I never claimed to *know* that there is a God. I *believe* that there is a God because I maintain that there are good reasons (i.e., rendering the world intelligible) for this belief. As a medieval philosopher said, "If I knew God, I would be Him."

The fact that we live in a world that is, for the most part, orderly, and that our cognitive equipment is generally reliable, points to the trustworthiness of a Higher Power underlying this universe.

What do spiritual realities, which you accept, have to do with a Higher Power? Everything. That's where they originate.

Please let me know if there are any questions I have not answered. If there are, please state them again instead of referring to previous letters.

Looking forward to hearing from you.

Love to Sylvia.

All the best.

Your friend,

Bill

18

Finale

June 17, 1991

Dear Bill,

When you or I quote a well-known figure (Whitehead, Einstein, etc.) it is not meant to prove anything. I am sure that we can each muster enough "expert witnesses" to cancel each other out. I think that we use these experts to illustrate rather than to try to prove a point.

Your "stopping point" is a cosmic mind or agent, but you do not have one *fact* to justify your going beyond the law of nature. You have only your imagination.

You state that "Only a cosmic mind can explain *existence*." God does not explain existence except as a fairy tale. And how can a mind, cosmic or otherwise, create a physical universe? You are not going to rely on God's omnipotence, are you? Can God create a rock so large that He cannot lift it?

Your statement "The feeling of dependence on a Higher Power is both learned and innate" is gratuitous and completely without substantiation. The universality of religion can be explained very simply by man's fear of and desire to control the forces of nature.

If you state (as you do in your letter) that God always existed, then you accept the concept of "infinity in both directions." That brings you one step closer to my feeling about the universe. And if the universe is infinite in both directions, what is the necessity of postulating a miracle to explain it?

I am sure that you know as many unethical religious people as unethical atheists, and as many ethical atheists as ethical religious people. Religion does not make people ethical. That is one of my arguments against it. After all the millennia, man is as unethical as he ever was. Religion is a failure.

If the *only* miracle that you believe is that of creation (or existence), how do you explain the manner in which God transmitted his ethical code to man? If none of the miraculous biblical conversations between God and man really happened (remember! only *one* miracle), how did man learn right from wrong from God?

If murder, stealing, lying, etc., were evil *per se*, then God did not differentiate them from honesty, charity, humanity, etc. They were different *per se*. If, on the other hand, the virtues were not different from the vices, then God would have had to make them so. Did God find the virtues different from the vices and simply tell man about the differences, or did He make them different? In either case, many difficult questions for the believer are raised.

Did God invent vice? Did God simply inform man of what was vice? I will not go further, but I think that you can see the ramifications of believing that God handed man his ethical code.

There is one God for all humanity. Right? Why then do ethical codes vary from culture to culture?

You state, "I think it makes more sense to attribute the ultimate origin of whatever ethical sense man has . . . to a Higher Power." I don't think it makes any sense at all, particularly in view of the "one miracle argument" and the paragraph comparing the virtues and vices (above). Man didn't learn ethics. He invented ethics. It was simply a matter of my not stealing your wife if you don't steal mine. It is simply a matter of "the social contract."

I particularly enjoyed your paragraph on "intelligibility" because I feel that I can riddle it full of holes. Let's start with both of *Webster's* definitions: intelligible—(1) capable of being understood or comprehended; (2) apprehensible by intellect alone. When the wind blows in the trees in late Autumn, the leaves fall to the ground in a "chance" pattern, a pattern without apparent cause or design. But this *chance* pattern, while obviously without apparent cause or design, is *not* unexplained or unintelligible. It is readily explained and easily understood. All this, even though the layout of the leaves is random and clearly determined by chance. My *Webster's* calls "chance" something that happens unpredictably without discernible human intention or observable cause.

Since the dawn of the scientific age, the universe has been in process of being understood. It has been a slow, gradual process, but every year more and more of the so-called secrets of the universe give up their secrecy. In other words, every year the universe becomes more intelligible (more understood) *without benefit of Deity.*

Examine the sentence "If I knew God, I would be Him" from a detached, nontheologian, nonsecular position. What in God's name does it mean? (From a grammatical position, it is incorrect. It should read, "If I knew God, I would be He.")

May I take the liberty of modifying your paragraph on the orderly world? The fact that we live in a world that is, for the most part, orderly and that our cognitive equipment is in general reliable points to the untrustworthiness of a Higher Power underlying this universe. Bill, I am not trying to be funny. I am simply trying to point out that your statement is totally without support in fact—just as is my modification.

If spiritual realities come from a Higher Power (as you state), by what means do they come? By what miracle did God transmit these spiritual realities to man? Another miracle? (Sorry, only one to a customer!) And where did I get my spiritual realities? Certainly, God does not talk to me!

Please try to answer *all* of the questions posed above.

I really don't know why you are looking forward to hearing from me. I'm so nasty to your God.

Love to the family.

Your friend,

Mort

June 24, 1991

Dear Mort,

In response to your letter of June 17, I don't mind that
you are being nasty to the Deity. As Elisabeth Kübler-
Ross (the "authority" on Death and Dying) said, in reference to suffering, dying patients cursing the Deity,
"He/She/It [i.e., the Deity] can take it [i.e., the cursing]."

I really am not out to defend God. He/She/It can take
care of Himself/Herself/Itself. And as one writer said, "If
God does not exist, that's His/Her/Its problem."

All I am trying to show is that the atheist's position (i.e.,
your position) is *not* intellectually superior to my position (i.e., the theist's position).

I agree with your point about experts. However, there is
one expert you absolutely must read. Please read the
book by the physicist Freeman Dyson, entitled *Infinite
in All Directions*.[1]

As the title of the book indicates, Dyson, like yourself,
holds that the universe is infinite in all directions. But
like me, he says that the most astounding thing in the
universe is the power of mind. He states that he agrees
with the process philosopher Charles Hartshorne, that
God is inherent in the universe and growing in power
and knowledge as the universe unfolds. He maintains
that God is what mind becomes when it has passed be-

---

1. Freeman Dyson, *Infinite in All Directions* (New York: Harper and
Row, 1988).

yond the scale of our comprehension. Thus, for him, God is the World-Soul or World-Mind.

Now, in my opinion, God as cosmic mind or agent is a better stopping point than the physical universe itself. I have never observed anything physical creating itself. A law of nature is a description, not an act. An act of an agent or mind can be the only real explanation of the universe and existence. If there is no cosmic mind or agent, then the universe is just there, unexplained. Chance is not an explanation.

Therefore, what justifies me in going beyond the law of nature is the *fact* that a law of nature is not an explanation but a description. The notion of a cosmic mind or agent is an *inference* from that fact which, if it is true that this agent exists, would be an explanation. You have no more evidence that it's false than I have that it's true.

I am not at all sure that God is omnipotent. God may be growing in knowledge and power, as Dyson and Hartshorne maintain. All I am maintaining is that a Superior Intelligence, Mind, or Agent is a better, more rational, explanation for the complexity of the universe than no explanation.

The only phrase I can think of regarding simplicity is that the simplest explanation is the best. I agree that a law of nature is simpler than a Supreme Being, but a law of nature is *not* an explanation of the universe. A law of nature is a description of the universe, which cries out for an explanation.

My point about a feeling of dependence is not unsubstantiated. People are not idiots. We must respect this feeling of dependence that the majority of humankind has.

I am not postulating a miracle to explain the universe. I am saying that the universe, or existence itself, is a miracle that cries out for an explanation.

Neither religion nor anything else has made man ethical. Perhaps not religion, but man is a failure. Maybe the Christians are right about original sin.

I do not pretend to understand what the biblical phrase "God spoke" meant. My belief is that without guidance from a Higher Power, there would be no ethics whatsoever; man would be a total beast. Guidance by a Higher Power is not what I mean by a miracle. A miracle to me means a suspension of natural law (such as the alleged miracle at the Red Sea). For me, God works *through* the laws of nature, not by overturning them. But why are there laws of nature at all? Why is there a universe? Why do we exist? The whole thing—existence, the universe, the totality of natural laws—cannot be *explained* by a natural law. That's why the existence of the whole thing is the only miracle. If scientists succeed in finding a universal formula (a theory of everything), that still would not explain *why* there is a universe, *why* we exist, etc.

Laws of nature and increasing scientific knowledge of them do indeed render the *operation* of the universe more intelligible. But they don't go an inch toward explaining *why* there is a universe. That's why we need a Deity as a source of explanation for the reason or reasons for the existence of a universe or universes.

Our minds are finite. God's mind, if God exists, is infinite. If I knew the contents of such a Universal Mind, I would be it. This does make sense.

Again, I do not *know* that there is a God, a Universal Mind. I *believe* that there is, because without it, the reason for the universe and for my existence isn't intelligible.

You are not bothered by this unintelligibility. I am. That's where we differ. For me, God is our ultimate hope.

Incidentally, you asked a good question. Where do you get *your* spiritual realities from?

Looking forward to your continuing nastiness to the Deity. He/She/It can take it.

Love to Sylvia.

> Your friend,
>
> Bill

03 03 80 80

June 19, 1991

Dear Bill,

I have finally had the time to sit down and go back over our correspondence to find the questions which I have raised which you have not answered. I have only gone back to the beginning of May.

Letter of May 8
¶3 Why do believers always answer difficult or impossible questions by postulating a HP? Does doing good necessarily imply a HP?
¶6 What is the difference between a logical and a scientific sense?

Letter of May 13

¶6 Do you seriously mean that we should accept the concept of God because it has been around for so many millennia?

Letter of May 16

¶4 1. Why do you assume that a Supreme Being who has permitted such horrendous events to befall man . . . is trustworthy?
    2. What is the connection between the reliability of my cognitive faculties and a "trustworthy" Supreme Being?

¶3 2. How do you *know* that He created us in His image?
    3. How do you know that the image includes the capacity to reason?

Letter of May 21

¶2 1. What has "humanistic knowledge" got to do with a Higher Power?
    2. What has "spiritual realism" got to do with a Higher Power?

¶3 What do you mean by an external world?

¶4 Do you apply strict rules of logic to everything except philosophical concepts and think of philosophy in terms of faith, belief, and nonrational ideation?

Letter of May 25

¶2 What is the meaning of your phrase "the harmony between our minds and the world"?

¶5 Are you going back to our anthropomorphic God who made man in his image and gave him free will? Did God make a serious error in so doing?

¶9 What about the logic you apply to my seven-legged dog being applied to the Soviet's two-headed dog?

Letter of June 17

¶5   If the universe is "infinite in all directions," why is it necessary to postulate a miracle to explain it?

¶7   If there was only one miracle, and that was the creation, how did man learn right from wrong from God?

¶9   If there is one God for all of humanity and God gave man his ethical code, how come that code varies from culture to culture?

And finally, atop page 2, the paragraph which begins, "If murder, stealing, lying, etc., . . .": Will you please refute the logic in this paragraph?

This should keep you busy for a while.

Enjoy!

Your friend,

Mort

ങ ങ ഒ ഒ

June 19, 1991

Dear Bill,

This is not a response to any of your letters. It is, rather, laying out for you a few of the thoughts that I had the other day.

I was thinking about the various explanations of God as propounded by Mordecai Kaplan, Hartshorne, White-head, et al. I consider myself a man of above-average intelligence and I have difficulty grasping many of the ideas of the theologians. If I have difficulty with these concepts, what hope is there that the masses of people will accept and understand these abstruse, complex philosophical concepts? And if they find these concepts of God incomprehensible, of what significance and of what use are these God ideas to them? Of what use is this God to them?

If, on the other hand, religious leaders digest, simplify, and sugarcoat these God-concepts to make them more easily digestible and assimilable, are we not justified in saying that a hoax is being perpetrated on the people by the rabbis, priests, and imams?

What is the connection between the God(s) of our theologians and the God that is worshiped at Temple Beth El in Fall River, Massachusetts? What percentage of your congregation would understand and accept these ideas of God?

If you accept the point that I am trying to make, how do you respond to it?

All the best to the family.

Your friend,

Mort

ભ ભ ৪৩ ৪৩

June 21, 1991

Dear Bill,

I wish to reply to only one point, as it is so basic to our discussion. You state, as you have several times in the past, that my assumption that there is no God is as much a presupposition as your belief that there is. I deny this, as I have each time you have made this point. I think that my cogent response to you was in my letter of May 16, and I quote:

> As I have stated repeatedly, I cannot prove the nonexistence of God, nor can I prove the nonexistence of the dog with seven legs. I cannot (and I do not) deny the existence of either. I simply state that lacking IVE of any kind I will assume that neither of them exists, until such time as IVE of the existence of either of them is presented.

When we started our dialogue, I was a confirmed atheist. I believed in a mechanistic universe. I never had the opportunity of testing my ideas except against those whose theism was based on blind faith. Our dialogue has been, for me, a unique experience. It made me think more critically about my ideas. It made me listen to and analyze opposing ideas, ideas which formerly I might simply have rejected out of hand without any thought. For the first time, I was exposed to theology as opposed to blind faith.

The result of all of this is that I now feel that my ideas about God have stood the test of fire. I am more firmly convinced than ever that belief in the existence of God is a chimera.

What, if anything, has exposure to my ideas and arguments done to your belief?

I await your reply with intense interest.

Your friend,

Mort

 св св во во

June 24, 1991

Dear Mort,

Let me try to answer some of your questions. First, of June 19:

1. Believers do not always answer difficult or impossible questions by postulating a Higher Power. Doing good does not necessarily imply a HP. What I wanted you to think about was the idea that the ultimate source of morality is a HP.

2. Scientific reasoning is generally inductive (from particular instances to general laws). Logic generally is both deductive (from general to particular) and inductive.

3. One of the arguments for the existence of God is known as the argument from the common consent of humankind. I don't think it's a decisive proof, but it does indicate that we ought to examine the concept of God seriously, since it has been around so many millennia.

4. God is trustworthy, in my opinion, mainly in the sense that He has created a world with reliable natural laws which the human mind can understand (for the most part). Natural evil is a result of chance, moral evil a result of man's misuse of his freedom. The order and trustworthiness that does exist in our universe, I believe, is due to God.

5. As I have repeated many times, I know nothing about God. I *believe* that God exists because, at present, I believe the religious hypothesis (i.e., God) is the best explanation of the universe. Just as your view is subject to revision if you discover IVE, so is my view subject to revision if I find by IVE that there is no Deity. I haven't as yet been convinced by the atheist.

6. As I remember, the phrases "humanistic knowledge" and "spiritual realism" were used by Christopher Lasch in the article you sent me.

7. By an external world, I mean a world independent of you, Mort Shor, perceiving it. Can you prove that it exists?

8. We have to start somewhere, with axioms, intuitions, etc. I would use terms like these with respect to philosophy rather than faith.

9. The harmony of our minds and the world means our ability to understand the world insofar as we do.

10. Our talk about God, for the most part, is metaphorical. We can't avoid using anthropomorphisms.

11. What's the point about a seven-legged dog and the Soviet's two-headed dog?

12. Again, I know nothing about God.

I posit and hope for an ultimate meaning. "God knows" is a metaphor for "the whole thing makes sense."

13. Can you answer the question, Why does the universe exist? The only answer, if there is one, takes us into the realm of miracle and mystery. The original impulse for good I believe comes from God; it is developed by human beings with cultural variations.

Concerning your letter of June 20th: You leave me no room to maneuver.

If I try to develop a notion of God tenable for the modern/postmodern mind, it's too complex and abstruse.

If I defend the traditional notion, I'm perpetuating a hoax.

I have enjoyed our dialogue immensely. You have given me a taste for IVE.

Unlike your confirmed atheism, my theism is quite tentative, always subject to revision. I acknowledge that you *may* be right. You have never said that I *might* be right. I think I am open-minded in my theism. You present the atheist's position more dogmatically than I expound theism.

Your friend,

Bill

19

Reflections on Faith and Reason

INTRODUCTORY COMMENT TO
REFLECTIONS ON FAITH AND REASON

The final series of letters between Rabbi Kaufman and Mort Shor deals with the issue of faith and reason.

What is faith?

Faith, in the sense of the Hebrew Bible, is trust or confidence in the will and the promise of God. It is an existential attitude of the total person, a life centered on belief in a personal God.

Under the influence of the Greeks, faith took on the connotation of assent to certain propositions as true, of believing that God exists, that God cares about us, etc. Clearly, belief in God is predicated upon belief that God exists, but faith was not formulated in terms of "belief-that" propositions until religious thinkers came under the influence of Greek philosophy.

Clearly, there are degrees of faith.

Rabbi Kaufman represents a faith in dialogue with reason. Dr. Kaufman holds that it is important for human beings to strike the right balance of belief. One can err by believing too much or too little. The individual who believes too much suffers from gullibility or credulity; the person who believes too little is guilty of excessive incredulity or skepticism. If you believe too much, your mind will be cluttered with falsehoods. If you believe too little, you may deprive yourself of much valuable information. The creative median between credulity and skepticism is a rational faith, that is, a faith which is not contrary to reason. To be sure, faith goes beyond reason as a dotted line in the direction to which reason points, and not as a jagged, irrational tangent. In short, it is Rabbi Kaufman's contention that faith opens up dimensions and possibilities that are closed to one who refuses to go beyond observable, verifiable experience. Thus, Rabbi Kaufman occupies an intermediate position between those who are willing to accept the "whole religious package" on faith and those who refuse to take anything on faith. Rabbi Kaufman's position is one of faith seeking understanding, faith in dialogue with reason.

It is important to recognize that Rabbi Kaufman's position is only one of many varieties of faith in contemporary Jewish life. There is, for example, faith as total unwavering commitment, espoused, for example, by the Orthodox Jewish theologian Norman Lamm. Lamm, in his book *Faith and Doubt*, allows for the legitimacy of doubt with respect to cognitive faith but claims that without "a total commitment to *Halakhah* as divine law and as the binding normative expression of Judaism, doubt loses its religious value."[1] In short, according to Lamm, a functional faith must be absolute and unconditional, even while doubt continues to play a role in cognitive faith—the role of questioning and exploring issues concerning some aspects of the nature of God. What *cannot* be doubted, according to this Orthodox thinker, is that the Jewish law—the *Halakhah*—is God-given.

So, too, many fundamentalist Christians have a total, absolute, and

---

1. Norman Lamm, *Faith and Doubt* (New York: Ktav Publishing House, Inc. 1971), p. 21.

unconditional faith that the Bible is the literal word of God and is therefore true in every respect.

An individual of total, unwavering, unconditional, and unquestioning faith would probably not be willing to expose his or her views to the scrutiny of an atheist like Mort Shor. After the first exchange of letters, the positions of totalistic faith and atheism would be hardened and congealed with no room for dialogue.

To be sure, many people go through life with a faith or total commitment which they do not examine as incessantly as Rabbi Kaufman does. However, Rabbi Kaufman does have a *core* of unquestioning faith; throughout the correspondence, Kaufman holds to an unwavering and undeviating commitment to belief that there *is* a Higher Power, a God. He could not be a practicing rabbi if he didn't hold this commitment. However, unlike the fundamentalist, Kaufman has studied enough philosophy and theology to realize that there are a variety of God-concepts. His *faith* lies in holding to his commitment as the foundation of his life, despite the fact that he may not be able to justify it to the satisfaction of skeptical philosophers. Again, his is a faith *seeking* understanding and justification: a lifelong quest.

C? C? ?? ??

September 21, 1992

Dear Mort,

In our discussions so far, I don't think that we've devoted enough attention to the phenomenon of faith.

I remember a lecture given by Max Dimont, author of *Jews, God, and History*, in which he commented that history has been shaped by men of faith more than by philosophers. Of course, faith has led to religious wars, but think of the positive teachings of Moses, Jesus, Buddha, etc.

Since you like the dictionary, let's take a look at the meanings of faith in *Webster's New World Dictionary*:

1. Unquestioning belief that does not require proof or evidence

2. Unquestioning belief in God, religious tenets, etc.

3. A religion or system of religious beliefs

4. Anything believed

5. Complete trust, confidence, or reliance

6. Allegiance to some person or thing

Faith is not the same as belief. Belief implies mental acceptance of something as true, even though absolute certainty may be absent. Faith implies complete, unquestioning acceptance of something even in the absence of proof and, especially, of something not supported by reason.

Clearly, there must be a role for faith in the scheme of things. It's probably necessary for life!

What do you have faith in? How do you understand the phenomenon of religious faith?

Have a good time in Vancouver.

Your friend,

Bill

June 21, 1991

Dear Bill,

Before we proceed further, let us agree upon our definitions. I think that you will accept my *Webster's* on belief and faith.

> belief: conviction of the truth of some statement or reality of fact, especially when well grounded

> faith: firm belief in something for which there is no proof

Taking the claims you make for and about faith one by one: You ask me to think of the positive teachings of the great religious leaders (Moses, Jesus, Buddha, etc.). My position is that the moral precepts expounded by these great thinkers were simply expressions of the social contract, i.e., if you don't steal my cow, I won't steal yours. Or better: Don't steal my cow and I won't steal yours.

You go on to make two statements that are totally unsupported by fact. Obviously, to you they are matters of faith (something for which there is no proof). You say, "Clearly, there must be a role for faith in the scheme of things. It's probably a necessity for life!" Why must there be a role for faith? Why do you think it is necessary to life? This is another example of the compartmentalization of the mind of the believer. In all matters outside of faith you use logic and reason. When it comes to faith, you have a separate compartment in your mind which operates on faith only.

In the strict definition listed above, I have faith in nothing. In the broader definitions (which do not apply here) I have faith in many things: my wife's love, the warmth of my friends, etc. But that has nothing to do with faith in the sense that we use it.

How do I understand the phenomenon of religious faith? Ignorance, fear, prejudice, all of the negatives that a God-fearing parent can breed into a child.

How do you explain the phenomenon of religious faith?

Love to the family.

Your friend,

Mort

CƷ CƷ Ꝋ Ꝋ

October 26, 1992

Dear Mort,

In your previous letter, you objected to my statement "Clearly, there must be a role for faith in the scheme of things. It's probably a necessity for life."

You explain your objection as follows: "Why must there be a role for faith? Why do you think it is necessary to life? This is another example of the compartmentalization of the mind of the believer. In all matters outside of faith you use logic and reason. When it comes to faith, you have a separate compartment in your mind which operates on faith only."

Here is my reply:

You state that "in all matters outside of faith you use logic and reason." This is psychologically incorrect and unsound. Psychiatrist Willard Gaylin, in his book *The Rage Within: Anger in Modern Life*, explains: "Contrary to much popular literature which sees feelings as opposite or alternative to rationality, they are instruments of reasoning . . . a form of fine-tuning."[2]

No, we human beings do not operate exclusively on logic and reason, but rather on logic and reason in concert with feelings. Similarly, the religious life is an interplay between faith and reason. The proper religious attitude, underscored by the medieval philosopher Anselm, is "faith seeking understanding"—faith cooperating with reason.

We wouldn't get very far in life without faith. Let us define faith as "the readiness to believe that which cannot be completely proved." Philosophically we cannot prove the objective reality of the external world. Yet we live on the basis of an "animal faith" that our senses are basically trustworthy.

Similarly, although we cannot prove the existence of God, life forces us to take a position. Theoretically, one can be agnostic. Practically, one decides either for or against God. The religious individual decides to base his life on faith in God, thus interpreting reality as the manifestation of a Supreme Being, Spirit or Mind-Energy. Acting on faith, the individual may experience

---

2. Willard Gaylin, *The Rage Within: Anger in Modern Life* (New York: Penguin Books, 1989), p. 21.

features of reality—such as the sublime, the mystery, the awesomeness of the universe—which otherwise he or she would not notice. Thus, the rational justification of acting on faith is that spiritual aspects of reality become open to one, to which one would otherwise be closed.

Personally, I have faith in the existence of God. I utilize reason to develop a concept of the nature of God. My belief is that faith takes us beyond reason but is not contrary to reason. Faith must be consistent with the reasonable and the known, like a dotted line that continues in the general direction of reason, not one which goes off at a capricious or contradictory angle. For example, it is logically possible that the universe is self-existent. But it is not rationally plausible, for we find nothing about the world to suggest that it exists by its own nature. Thus, although we cannot prove that God created the universe, it is at least as reasonable, if not more rational, to act on the faith that God created it.

Hence, I explain the phenomenon of faith to be a result of the psychological necessity I and most people experience to have an orientation to or interpretation of reality as a whole, which functions as a guide for my life.

Don't you have faith in the omnicompetence of science, that for every question one can eventually find independently verifiable evidence? Isn't this a "firm belief in something for which there is no proof," namely, that science can explain everything?

If not this, don't you live by faith in something? Do you really have "faith in nothing"?

I look forward to your response to my explanation of faith and my questions to you.

Love to Sylvia.

Your friend,

Bill

ભ ભ ભ ભ

October 28, 1992

Dear Bill,

You start your letter of October 26 by referring to the role of faith in life. You then switch over to feelings. Let us first make certain that we agree on the meaning of the word *faith*. In dealing with religion, the word *faith* means not only a belief that does not require proof of any kind but a belief for which the attempt to assign proof dilutes the meaning of the word. Faith also means confidence, as in, "I have faith that the sun will rise in the East tomorrow morning."

Now, back to faith and feelings. You quote Dr. Gaylin as saying that feelings are the instruments of reasoning and are a form of fine-tuning. To me this sounds like just so many words without real meaning. What is an instrument of reasoning? What is being fine-tuned? How is the fine-tuning brought about? And finally, I thought that we had agreed that we could each find "expert witnesses" to support our positions and that these experts would cancel each other out.

Of course, you are right, we human beings do not operate exclusively on logic and reason. But it is when we allow our feelings to dilute (or negate) our logic that we really get into the most trouble. The vast majority of marriages are based on feelings, not on reason. Over 50 percent end in divorce. Everyone knows that the use of drugs leads to addiction, probably prison, and possibly death. But the lure of drugs is to feelings. And drug use continues to increase. Crimes of passion are based upon feelings, not on reason. You cannot seriously believe that feelings are a wiser guide to life than reason!

You say that the religious life is an interplay between faith and reason. Remember a basic law of logic: If you start with a false assumption and use perfect logic, you must arrive at a false conclusion. I am not arguing the place of logic in religion—although I am not quite sure what it is. I simply state that your assuming God is your false assumption and, thus, your conclusions must be false.

I also do not disagree with Anselm. As you say, he states that the proper religious attitude is "faith seeking understanding." He postulates faith. He assumes faith. He does not explain it, justify it, or prove it. Faith is his initial false assumption.

You state that we couldn't get very far in life without faith. Using your definition of the word, I reject this statement *in toto*. If you accept my definition (confidence) I'll agree. I have gotten *very* far in life without the faith that you describe.

I cannot even accept your definition of your kind of faith unless you delete the word *completely*. I will accept that your word *faith* means the readiness to believe that which cannot be proved.

We live on the *assumption* that the external world is real only so long as we agree on what we see, hear, smell, taste, and feel. (It is when we start fooling around with that sixth sense that we get into matters of faith [in your sense of the word].) It doesn't really matter whether the evidence of our senses is true or not, as long as we all agree. It is conceivable that we all have red-tinted lenses in our eyes and that the "real" colors of the world may differ from what we see. As long as we identify the colors by their respective wavelengths, it does not matter how we see them—as long as we all see them the same. As a practical matter, however, we assume that what we see is correct. This is practicality, not faith.

You state that life forces us to take a position on the existence of God. I disagree. Life doesn't force us. You and the other theists force us to take a position. Life doesn't force us to take a position on seven-legged dogs. If, however, there were a worldwide movement that believed in the existence of these monsters and, perhaps, worshiped them, then we would be forced to take a position.

Do you really believe that only believers can "experience features of reality—such as the sublime, the mystery, the awesomeness of the universe . . ."? The astrophysicist, the astronomer, and the scientist, who certainly know a good deal more about the matter, probably have deeper feelings of awe at the beauty and mystery of the cosmos than the theist who simply has blind faith. A belief in God is not needed to experience these feelings. It may, in fact, mask or dull them.

Is it more reasonable to believe that God created the universe than to believe that it always existed? And if God is a force (Kaplan) or a process (Whitehead), how does a force or a process create anything from nothing? And, of course, whence the force or process?

As you say, faith is a psychological necessity of most people. Centuries ago people believed that the earth was the center of the universe—and that it was flat. What most people believe, want, or need is not a measure of what is correct or what is right. (See Germany, 1933 to 1945.)

When I say that I have faith in science, I use the word *faith* as in the sentence, "I have faith that if I throw a stone into the air it will fall to the ground unless acted upon by some other agency." This is confidence based upon past experience. It is not belief in something that cannot be proven. Your use of the word *faith* has nothing to do with experience or proof. In fact, proof and faith are mutually exclusive.

You ask if I do not have faith in anything. Yes, I have faith in many things, but not in the sense in which you use the word. I have faith in the people whom I love and who love me. I have faith in the goodness of man—not innate but taught. I have faith that science will continue to solve the mysteries of the cosmos. All of them? I don't know. But here, again, a better word might be *confidence*, confidence based upon past experience.

Perhaps I have been too wordy in trying to clarify where you and I differ, but I had to make clear that when I have faith it means something utterly different from your saying the same words.

Shall we go on, good friend?

All the best to Nathalie and the children.

Your friend,

Mort

ভ্চ ভ্চ ৪০ ৪০

November 6, 1992

Dear Mort,

You are quite right about the two meanings of "faith" you suggest:

1. Confidence

2. A belief that does not require proof of any kind

The contemporary Jewish philosopher Martin Buber, in his book *Two Types of Faith*, delineates two basic forms of faith: "the one from the fact that I trust someone, without being able to offer sufficient reasons for my trust in him; the other from the fact that, likewise without being able to give sufficient reason, I acknowledge a thing to be true."[3]

The first type of faith is generally known as "belief *in*" someone or something, the second as "belief *that*" something is true or is the case.

I would also make another distinction. There are those who *start* with a leap of faith or total commitment. Some

---

3. Martin Buber, *Two Types of Faith*, trans. Norman P. Goldhawk (New York: Harper Torchbook edition, 1961), p. 7.

believe in "blind faith" or take an irrational leap of faith (as the medieval church father Tertullian, who said "I believe because it is absurd"—referring to Christian doctrines such as the Incarnation or the Resurrection).

As a Jew, I do not subscribe to irrational faith (faith contrary to reason). Some Jews, such as Orthodox, do make an *initial* nonrational (beyond reason) commitment. Orthodox thinker Norman Lamm, professor of Jewish philosophy at Yeshiva University, begins with what he calls *functional faith*—an absolute and unconditional "total commitment to *Halakhah* [Jewish law] as divine law and as the binding normative expression of Judaism," even though he allows for doubts on the cognitive level.[4]

My own position, as I have said, is that faith takes us beyond reason but should not be contrary to reason. Faith must be consistent with the reasonable and the known, like a dotted line that continues in the general direction of reason, not one which goes off at a capricious or contradictory angle. Unlike most Orthodox thinkers, I begin with reason, discover its limits, and then act on faith.

Clearly, you rule out the role of faith entirely when you say to me that "your assuming God is your false assumption and, thus, your conclusions must be false."

Here you are simply begging the question. I agree with the American philosopher William James, who in his famous essay *The Will to Believe* said that we are rationally entitled to believe in God, because living by this

---

4. Lamm, *Faith and Doubt*, p. 21.

belief may open us up to spiritual realities that we may not otherwise experience. The atheist, too, makes an emotional decision and takes a risk in losing this dimension, if it exists, just as the religious individual takes a risk that he or she might be wrong, if this dimension does not exist.

Won't you admit that you just *might* be wrong, that assuming God *may be* the correct assumption? Your dogmatic certainty about atheism exceeds my dogmatic certainty about theism.

But my blend of faith and reason is only one of the many *varieties of faith*. Some are as *certain* about their faith as you are about atheism.

How do you react to that phenomenon?

I look forward to hearing from you.

Sincerely, your friend,

Bill

ឥ ឥ ឦ ឦ

November 10, 1992

Dear Bill,

I see little difference between Buber's "Two Types of Faith" as explained in your letter of November 6. The Brooklyn Bridge has been sold too many times by someone being trusted without sufficient reason. And I feel that the Brooklyn Bridge is being bought again by those who put their faith in God.

Both of your kinds of faith are really the same thing: putting trust in a person or a belief without proof, *or the necessity of proof*. If you will refer back to my last letter, you will find that I point out two very distinctly different meanings of the word *faith*:

1. Faith is the belief in a person or an alleged fact without proof or the necessity of proof (God, for example).

2. Faith is confidence in a person or fact based upon previous experience (the daily rising of the sun or the honesty of my friend Rabbi Kaufman, for example).

I find it difficult to accept your statement, "As a Jew, I do not subscribe to irrational faith (faith contrary to reason)." Your faith in God is totally unsupported by reason.

Your paragraph which begins, "My own position, as I have said, is that faith takes us beyond reason . . ." leaves me open-mouthed. I can only respond with questions:

1. What does it mean to say that faith takes us beyond reason?

2. Can I assume that you mean that there is no connection between faith and reason?

3. What on Earth is the connection between faith in the existence of God (Person, Thing, Process, or Whatever) and reason?

4. If you begin with reason, as you say, when (and how) do you make the "leap of faith"? In other words, when do you suspend reason?

I must disagree with your expert witness William James when he says that we are rationally entitled to believe in God. If you drop the word *rationally*, we can agree. And what spiritual realities (other than visions of the Blessed Virgin) does he mean? Also, what is a spiritual reality? (No more expert witnesses?)

I reject your statement that the atheist makes an emotional decision when he chooses atheism. My decision is based on the absence of any shred of independently verifiable evidence of the existence of God. Where does emotion enter into this?

I freely admit that I might be wrong about the existence of God, just as I might be wrong about the existence of a breed of dogs with seven legs.

And finally you ask how I react to the phenomenon that some believers are as certain of their faith as I am of my atheism. Very simply, the fact that the vast majority of people believe in something bears no relationship to fact. Everyone believed that the earth was the center of the universe—and only last week, the Vatican acknowledged that Galileo was right. There was a time when everyone believed the earth to be flat. There was a time when everyone believed God to be an old gentleman with a long white beard and flowing robes. In more recent times, *The New York Times* published the results of a Gallup poll of American adults which showed that about 70 percent of them believed in a rewarding Heaven and a punishing Hell after death. What difference does it make to reality what most people believe when the belief is unsupported by fact but *is* based upon faith?

On a personal note, Bill, it is important for you to know my attitude toward believers. I do not look down upon them or sneer at them. I feel that for many the need for faith is very great. Everyone is entitled to his or her belief or nonbelief.

So where do we go from here?

Love to the family.

Your friend,

Mort

ය ය ඞ ඞ

November 19, 1992

Dear Mort,

In answer to your questions, let me elucidate again some of the distinctions I am making.

First, I distinguish between the rational, the nonrational, and the irrational. The rational is what a reasonable person would accept. The nonrational is beyond reason but not contrary to reason (e.g., the existence of a Supreme Being). The irrational, which as a Jew I do not accept, is a doctrine that is *contrary* to reason (e.g., the Trinity—God is one but also three).

Second, let me explain again the relation between reason and faith, in my view.

On the basis of *reason*, I *infer* that it is more probable that the universe is the product of a Divine purposeful mind than a random accident. The reasoning I reject is the claim that if a large enough group of monkeys were trained to sit at typewriters, pounding their keys at random over a sufficiently long period of centuries, eventually one of them by sheer chance would succeed in typing out the Bible.

Thus, the position I reject is *your* position, that the entire universe is a product of chance. Of course, your position is logically possible. But my position is probable, that is, I think that it is more probable that the universe is the product of a Supreme intelligence than a consequence of chance. *Probability* seems to me to be a lot closer to truth than possibility.

Now, on the basis of "probable cause" (a legal, as well as a philosophical, concept), I then am willing, as an act of *faith*, to live on the basis of the premise that such a Supreme Being exists. Thus, it has been said that "probability is the very guide of life."

For me, the order of the universe points to the existence of a preeminent ordering entity or God. I believe it is more probable that such an ordering entity exists than to think, as you do, that the universe is totally a product of chance. Thus, my faith is an extrapolation from reason and not an abandonment of reason.

Concerning the definition of a spiritual reality, I mean the reality of the unseen: the sense of a Higher Power and presence when I experience the beauty and grandeur of the universe, the genius of artistic creation, and the Hebrew genius for ethical ideals.

Look forward to hearing from you.

Love to Sylvia!

Your friend,

Bill

C03 C03 80 80

November 21, 1992

Dear Bill,

I was sorely tempted to let your letter of November 19 be the "last word" in our discussion. On rereading it, however, I notice that several points you make cannot be left unchallenged.

First, you start your letter with, "In answer to your questions . . . ," but nowhere in your letter do you answer my four questions (*fier kashas*?)[5]

Second, you make the unsupported statement "that it is more probable that the universe is the product of a Divine purposeful mind than a random accident." Why is it more probable? And even if it were more probable, might I then quote you as saying, "There probably is a God"?

Third, I have read and reread your paragraph which begins "On the basis of reasoning to God" three or four times. Frankly, Bill, I don't understand what you are saying.

---

5. The traditional four questions that start the Passover *seder*.

Fourth, as you know, the vast majority of the women whom I counsel at the jail are incarcerated for drug-related offenses. Many of them have described the "high" which drugs give them in terms very close to your description of "spiritual reality."

Now what?

Your friend,

Mort

P.S. I still think that you should have the "last word."

ରଃ ରଃ ଚ୍ ଚ୍

December 10, 1992

Dear Mort,

I thought that I had answered your "four questions," but I'll be glad to try again.

1. What does it mean to say that faith takes us beyond reason?

Answer: Reason can only take us so far. Reason can show us the order and intricate design of the universe and lead us by an inference of probability to the idea of the Supreme Intelligence or Designer. But it requires a leap of faith (as a dotted line continuing in the same direction, not one going off on a capricious angle) to believe in a Supreme Being and to live by this belief. As you yourself imply, the locution "There probably is a God" is logically odd. That's why faith *must* take the religious man beyond the point where reason acknowledges its limits.

2. Can I assume that you mean that there is no connection between faith and reason?

Answer: No. I believe there is a connection. Faith must be a dotted line continuing in the same direction as reason but beyond reason, as I've indicated. However, as I shall soon point out, this is only *my* opinion and the opinion of other religious rationalists like myself. Others, called *fideists*, do believe in faith alone, as I shall soon illustrate.

3. What on Earth is the connection between faith in God and reason?

Answer: I've already explained it.

4. When do you suspend reason?

Answer: As I've indicated, where reason reaches its limits (i.e., ultimate issues, such as the meaning of life, and the religious need to go beyond probability).

The question whether we are rationally entitled to believe depends on how one defines rationality. I believe one is rationally entitled to believe in God, because it is reasonable to grant some force to the overwhelming testimony of prophets, mystics, and the like who have claimed to experience spiritual realities. Since you do not accept the testimony of "expert witness," I myself believe, with the poet Wordsworth, that there are "thoughts that lie too deep for tears." That is what *I* mean by spiritual realities.

You ask, where does emotion enter into it? You are emotionally committed to reason—to basing everything on independently verifiable evidence. That's an emotional commitment.

One final point: My faith, the faith of a religious ratio-
nalist, is only one type of faith. There are also those who
do say that there is *no* connection between faith and
reason. One such individual was the Russian novelist Leo
Tolstoy. Not having found what he was looking for (i.e.,
the meaning of life) in the great thinkers, he turned to
the huge masses of poor peasants. They drew their cour-
age from the most simple blind faith. Faith like theirs
could only be accepted, without question or argument.
One spring day, while he was walking in the forest, Tolstoy experienced this simple faith. "He wrote in his note-
book: 'The moment I thought I knew God, I lived. But,
the moment I forgot him, the moment I stopped believing, I also stopped living. . . . To know God and to live
are the same thing. God is life.' He had found faith. A
faith within reach of all."[6]

This is certainly not my approach, but there are those
who do hold to blind faith and find inner peace thereby.

Needless to say, I have enjoyed this correspondence, and
I certainly find your reasoning challenging and excit-
ing. But I simply do need a faith to live by, not a blind
faith, but a faith which goes beyond reason when reason
reaches its limits, a faith that is not contrary to reason.

Your friend,

Bill

---

6. Henri Troyat, *Tolstoy* (New York: Doubleday, 1967), p. 378.

III

EPILOGUES

20

Rabbi's Epilogue

My central argument is that the universe manifests an order and a complexity too striking to have occurred unexplained. It cries out for an explanation in terms of a unitary actuality, a Higher Power, a Universal Mind— a God.

My friend the atheist, Mort Shor, has come to recognize the human need for a God as an anodyne, a comforting hope that our existence has ultimate meaning and perhaps immortality. But he holds that the concept of God is *only* an idea—indeed, an inferior idea—a fiction on par with a seven-legged dog. When asked how he explains the universe, his reply is "chance."

Unlike the fundamentalist theist who claims that there is a Divine reason for everything, I hold with the process theist that chance is real. But chance is within limits, and these limits cannot be set by chance, for chance limited by chance would be sheer chaos. Rather, chance makes sense only against a framework of order. And the order of the universe, I believe, implies a preeminent cosmic Mind or Orderer.

There are not only first-rate philosophers, such as Charles Hartshorne, who hold this view. The physicist Freeman Dyson shares with Hartshorne the belief in an immanent God "inherent in the universe and growing in power and knowledge as the universe unfolds."[1] Dyson finds evidence of mind on three levels in the universe. The first of these is matter. Matter in quantum mechanics is not an inert substance but an active agent, constantly making choices between alternative possibilities according to probabilistic laws. The second level is the level of human existence. We human beings are the second big step in the development of mind.

It is therefore reasonable to believe in the existence of a third level of mind, a mental component of the universe, signifying that the universe as a whole is hospitable to mind. This is a metaphysical and not a scientific inference. I agree with Dyson that determining the laws of nature and the initial conditions for the universe is a metascientific or metaphysical issue beyond the scope of science.[2]

The difference between me and Mort Shor is that I am willing to extrapolate from our human experience metaphysical hypotheses such as God as the ultimate Mind, of which our mental apparatus is but a fragment. Mort Shor takes a strictly scientific stance, only allowing into play hypotheses that can be confirmed by in-

---

1. Freeman Dyson, *Infinite in All Directions* (New York: Harper and Row, 1988), p. 294.
2. Ibid., pp. 296, 297.

dependently verifiable evidence. I prefer the wider vision of a scientist like Dyson.

Mort is quite right that one cannot prove a vision or worldview. Rather, a worldview is presupposed in whatever we do. I have been trying to convince Mort Shor that he has a worldview too, that is, that he entertains basic presuppositions (such as the idea that matter and energy are ultimate). But I still don't think that he would allow that he has a worldview, he is simply convinced that this is the way things *are*–period.

That's the big difference between us. As a philosopher, I think in terms of visions and conceptual schemes. He refuses to go beyond what he considers to be the facts. I would not go so far as the philosopher Nietzsche, who said that there are no facts, only interpretations. But I do hold that facts are always within an interpretive or conceptual framework.

The conceptual framework I hold at the present time (always subject to revision, because I am ever open to new discoveries) is that the ultimate reality is a Universal Mind, a creative unitary actuality, a God. I believe this Universal Mind is the source of the world's order and of human creativity. Mozart writing symphonies at age eight, Beethoven composing them when he was deaf –these are dramatic examples to me of a Higher Power that nourishes the human mind. If the word *God* were in the same category as a seven-legged dog, not only would we have no world religions, but I don't think we would have a Mozart or a Beethoven either.

I am indebted to Mort Shor for adding to my critical awareness a new respect for facts and independently verifiable evidence. The religious significance of his atheism is that he cautions us to look before we take the leap of faith. He has succeeded in showing me that alternative concepts of God involve imaginative leaps similar to the act of faith in the omnipotent Supreme Being of classical theism. I have looked at the universe and am willing to extrapolate from my experience a Universal World-Mind in process with my experience and the world's. What I now realize through dialogue with Mort Shor is that the major question is whether ultimate reality is mind or matter—energy in motion. He holds to matter-energy; I hold to mind.

I believe that each of us is "a pulse in the mind of God." This is what the biblical idea of humans being created in the image of God means to me. We have indeed devised many and varied ideas of God, but I do not believe we have invented God. Our concepts are rather attempts and approximations to discover the God who has created us, in the sense of evoking the emergence of the human mind.

21

Atheist's Epilogue

And now we have come to the end of this disagreement, which will really never have an end. It all started out with two rather simple statements: "There is a God." "Really? Prove it." It seems to have become much more complicated. It is no longer a question of whether or not God exists. It has become a question of which God are we talking about and does He or doesn't He exist. Are we talking about the God of Abraham or of Muhammad? Is it Spinoza's God or Mordecai Kaplan's God? Are we talking about Hartshorne's or Whitehead's God? Or is it really William E. Kaufman's God? Is God a Being, a Thing, a Concept—or all of these or none of these? Is God a He, a She, or an It, or all of these or none of these? In our attempt to get some firm idea of God, I visualize the child playing with a droplet of mercury, trying to squash it with his thumb. The mercury slithers and slides uncontrollably. It cannot be made to stay put.

How is it, then, that despite this welter of God-concepts, and despite the abstruse, recondite nature of some
of them, the vast majority of mankind (probably in ex-
cess of 99 percent) believes in the existence of a Deity?
How is it that despite the absence of even the slightest
shred of IVE, belief in God's existence is almost total and
universal? And how is it that I have the unmitigated gall,
the unrelieved effrontery to pit my skepticism against
almost 100 percent of the world's population?

First, I put myself in the place of the man from outer
space that I referred to in my Prologue. I ask the questions: God? What is That? Who is That? Why do you
believe these things? Do you have any evidence to support these pictures of God that you have shown me? Why
are there so many different answers to the question of
what God is? Upon what do you base all of this? Then I
remember what Voltaire said, and that helps me with
some of my questions. He said, "If God did not exist, it
would have been necessary to invent Him." Man believes
because he has a desperate need to believe. He has a
craving, a hunger to believe. For the oppressed and the
dispossessed, belief in God gives some hope, some meaning to life where there is little or nothing else. Faith can
give a man the strength to bear the most onerous of bur-
dens.

But what of the relatively well off, the citizens of the
Western world? They are not oppressed. They live in rela-
tive affluence. Why do they overwhelmingly believe in
God? What is their need, their hunger?

How can a man accept the idea that he will live his
three-score-and-ten and then simply disappear into oblivion along with the countless millions who have gone
before? How can he read meaningfulness into his exis-

tence if the end is simply the end? Why was he placed on Earth? What is the value and the meaning of his life? What is the significance of his relationships with his loved ones? These and a myriad of other profound questions confront the thinking man. And there is a very simple answer to all of these questions—God. If man accepts God, all of his questions are answered. Not only does God give meaning to man's life here on Earth, but God also provides meaning for all of eternity. Belief in God implies the existence of the immortal soul and the concomitant belief (albeit frequently vague) in some kind of afterlife.[1]

So belief in God fulfills two purposes: it renders life on Earth worthwhile and meaningful, but possibly more important, it tells man that the end is not the end. How comforting to know that by fulfilling some divinely ordered purpose, one will have an eternal afterlife.

Is it any wonder then that man has invented God? If an imaginary God can bring meaning and purpose to life, then why not? If religion is the opiate of the masses, then so be it. Take the opiate, but recognize it for what it is. There is nothing wrong with opiates properly recognized and properly used. The early Jews worshiped the Golden Calf, their invention. Modern man worships God, his invention. Voltaire was right.

---

1. *The New York Times* of March 23, 1991 reported in the feature "Religion Notes" that the latest Gallup poll of Americans showed that 73 percent of the people polled believe that there is a place where people who had led good lives were eternally rewarded. On the subject of hell, 60 percent said they believed there was a place where those who led bad lives and died without repentance were eternally damned.

Bibliography

Bloom, Harold, and Rosenberg, David. *The Book of J.* New York: Grove Weidenfeld, 1990.

Buber, Martin. *Between Man and Man.* Trans. Ronald Gregor Smith. New York: Macmillan, 1978.

———. *Two Types of Faith.* Trans. Norman P. Goldhawk. New York: Harper Torchbook edition, 1961.

Cobb, John B., Jr. *A Christian Natural Theology.* Philadelphia: Westminster Press, 1965.

Dyson, Freeman. *Infinite in All Directions.* New York: Harper and Row, 1988.

Friedman, Richard. *Who Wrote the Bible?* New York: Harper and Row, 1987.

Fromm, Erich. *You Shall Be as Gods: A Radical Interpretation of the Old Testament and Its Traditions.* New York: Henry Holt & Co., 1991.

Gaylin, Willard, *The Rage Within: Anger in Modern Life.* New York: Penguin Books, 1989.

Ghiselin, Brewster, ed. *The Creative Process.* Berkeley, CA: University of California Press, 1952.

Gittelsohn, Roland. *Man's Best Hope*. New York: Random House, 1961.

Hartshorne, Charles. *The Logic of Perfection*. LaSalle, IL: Open Court Publishing Company, 1962.

Hertz, Joseph H. *The Authorized Daily Prayer Book*. Rev. ed. New York: Bloch Publishing Co., 1948.

Hick, John. *Philosophy of Religion*. 4th ed. Englewood Cliffs, NJ: Prentice Hall, 1990.

Hook, Sidney. *The Quest for Being*. Buffalo, NY: Prometheus Books, 1991.

James, William. *The Varieties of Religious Experience*. New York: Longmans, Green and Co., 1902.

——. *The Will to Believe and Other Essays*. New York: Longmans, 1987.

Kaplan, Mordecai M. *Judaism as a Civilization*. New York: Reconstructionist Press, 1957.

——. *The Future of the American Jew*. New York: Reconstructionist Press, 1967.

——. *The Meaning of God in Modern Jewish Religion*. New York: Reconstructionist Press, 1962.

——. *Judaism Without Supernaturalism*. New York: Reconstructionist Press, 1958.

Kaufman, William E. "The Relation of Man to the World in the Philosophy of John Wild." Ph.D. diss., Boston University, 1971.

——. *Contemporary Jewish Philosophies*. New York: Behrman House, Inc., and Reconstructionist Press, 1976. Reprinted 1985 by University Press of America, Lanham, MD, with a foreword by Jacob Neusner. Reprinted by Wayne State University Press, Detroit, MI, 1991.

——. *Journeys: An Introductory Guide to Jewish Mysticism*. New York: Bloch Publishing Co., 1980.

———. *The Case for God*. St. Louis, MO: The Chalice Press, 1991.

Kushner, Harold. *When Bad Things Happen to Good People*. New York: Schocken Books, 1981.

Lamm, Norman. *Faith and Doubt*. New York: Ktav Publishing House, Inc., 1971.

Lowe, Victor. *Understanding Whitehead*. Baltimore, MD: Johns Hopkins Press, 1966.

MacIntyre, Alasdair, and Ricoeur, Paul. *The Religious Significance of Atheism*. New York: Columbia University Press, 1969.

Otto, Rudolf. *The Idea of the Holy*. Trans. John W. Harvey. New York: Oxford University Press, 1958.

Sonsino, Rifat, and Syme, Daniel B. *Finding God: Ten Jewish Responses*. New York: Union of American Hebrew Congregations, 1986.

Steinberg, Milton. *Anatomy of Faith*. Ed. Arthur A. Cohen. New York: Harcourt, Brace Jovanovich, 1960.

———. *A Believing Jew*. New York: Harcourt, Brace Jovanovich, 1951.

Troyat, Henri. *Tolstoy*. New York: Doubleday, 1967.

Whitehead, Alfred North. *Science and the Modern World*. New York: The Free Press, 1953.

———. *Religion in the Making*. Cleveland, OH: World Publishing Co., 1960.

———. *Process and Reality*. Corrected edition ed. David Ray Griffin and Donald W. Sherburne. New York: The Free Press, 1978.

Index

About the Authors

William E. Kaufman is the rabbi at Temple Beth El in Fall River, Massachusetts, and an adjunct professor of philosophy at Rhode Island College. He received his rabbinic ordination from the Jewish Theological Seminary and a Ph.D. from Boston University. The author of *Contemporary Jewish Philosophies*, *The Case for God*, and *Journeys: An Introductory Guide to Jewish Mysticism*, his writings have appeared in many journals, including *Judaism*, *Conservative Judaism*, *The Reconstructionist*, and *The Jewish Spectator*. Rabbi Kaufman lives with his family in Massachusetts.

Morton Shor, now retired, for over forty years was the president of Shor International, a firm that imported and distributed machinery and tools for the manufacture of jewelry. He received a bachelor of chemical engineering degree from the City College of New York and pursued postgraduate work at Brooklyn Polytechnic Institute and Columbia University. Mr. Shor currently lives with his wife in Somers, New York.